ROMAN LEGENDS BROUGHT TO LIFE

In celebration of your
interest in the other
side of history.

Affectionately

[signature]

For Tony and Lorraine

I wish to express my deep gratitude to Paul Cartledge, who kindly agreed to read my manuscript at late stage and corrected many factual and stylistic errors with his customary grace and esprit – for such as remain I take full responsibility – and to Mike Goldmark and Mick Jagger, whose indefatigability and inspiration have been exemplary and determinative. Above all, I wish to thank Tony Aveni, my colleague at Colgate University, master equally of the anecdote and of the idea.

ROMAN LEGENDS BROUGHT TO LIFE

ROBERT GARLAND

PEN & SWORD
HISTORY

AN IMPRINT OF PEN & SWORD BOOKS LTD.
YORKSHIRE – PHILADELPHIA

First published in Great Britain in 2022 by
PEN AND SWORD HISTORY
An imprint of
Pen & Sword Books Ltd
Yorkshire – Philadelphia

Copyright © Robert Garland, 2022

ISBN 978 1 39909 852 6

A CIP catalogue record for this book is available from the British Library.

Typeset in Times New Roman 11.5/14 by SJmagic DESIGN SERVICES, India.
Printed and bound in the UK by CPI Group (UK) Ltd.

Pen & Sword Books Limited incorporates the imprints of Atlas, Archaeology,
Aviation, Discovery, Family History, Fiction, History, Maritime, Military, Military
Classics, Politics, Select, Transport, True Crime, Air World, Frontline Publishing,
Leo Cooper, Remember When, Seaforth Publishing, The Praetorian Press,
Wharncliffe Local History, Wharncliffe Transport, Wharncliffe True Crime and
White Owl.

For a complete list of Pen & Sword titles please contact
PEN & SWORD BOOKS LIMITED
47 Church Street, Barnsley, South Yorkshire, S70 2AS, England
E-mail: enquiries@pen-and-sword.co.uk
Website: www.pen-and-sword.co.uk

Or
PEN AND SWORD BOOKS
1950 Lawrence Rd, Havertown, PA 19083, USA
E-mail: Uspen-and-sword@casematepublishers.com
Website: www.penandswordbooks.com

Contents

A Mostly Somewhat Putative Chronology

All dates are BCE unless otherwise stated.

1150	Fall of Troy
753	Romulus founds Rome
716	Death of Romulus; accession of Numa Pompilius
673	Death of Numa Pompilius; accession of Tullus Hostilius
642	Death of Tullus Hostilius; accession of Ancus Marcius
617	Death of Ancus Marcius; accession of Tarquinius Priscus
579	Death of Tarquinius Priscus; accession of Servius Tullius
535	Death of Servius Tullius; accession of Tarquin the Proud
509	Tarquin the Proud is expelled from Rome; Brutus establishes the Republic
508	Mucius Scaevola attempts to kill Lars Porsena, king of Clusium; Cloelia swims to safety
493	Coriolanus defeats the Volscians
458	Cincinnatus is appointed dictator
449	Appius Claudius lusts after Verginia
396	Veii is destroyed
394	Camillus rejects an offer from the Falerian schoolteacher
387	The Romans are defeated at the Battle of the Allia; the Gauls sack Rome
384	Marcus Manlius is thrown from the Tarpeian Rock
340	Decius Mus sacrifices himself to the spirits of the dead
321	The Battle of the Caudine Forks
279	Pyrrhus wins a pyrrhic victory
249	Publius Claudius Pulcher fails to heed the warning from the sacred chickens and loses the Battle of Drepana
218	Hannibal crosses the Alps
216	Hannibal defeats the Romans at the Battle of Cannae

A Mostly Somewhat Putative Chronology

204	The Great Mother arrives in Rome
202	Hannibal is defeated at the Battle of Zama
172	Antiochus IV Epiphanes is humiliated
146	Carthage is destroyed
133	Assassination of Tiberius Gracchus
121	Assassination of Gaius Gracchus
107	Marius reforms the Roman army
81	Sulla becomes dictator
73–1	Revolt of Spartacus
49	Julius Caesar crosses the Rubicon
44	Julius Caesar is assassinated
27	Octavian becomes Augustus
CE 410	Alaric the Goth sacks Rome

Introduction and Prefatory Remarks

Myths Versus Legends

The Greeks exhibited an amazing aptitude for fashioning myths about gods and heroes. Not so the Romans, who failed to produce an independent mythological tradition. But what the Romans did excel at was in shaping legends about the men and women who were instrumental in giving their city its distinctive character in the first centuries of its existence.

In making this claim, I'm aware that many scholars eschew the word 'legend' altogether and prefer to classify as 'myth' any story told over the course of several generations that has significance for the community as a whole. I have chosen to keep the distinction between the two words. By my definition, whereas a myth is a story set in the remote past, that's to say, in an imaginary era when the world was still in its infancy and when gods and humans were in direct and regular contact with one another, a legend is set squarely in human history, irrespective of whether it is historical or fabricated. In making this distinction, I am not casting aspersions on the Roman imagination, which was in no way inferior to that of the Greeks in explaining the past. I am merely limiting the duration of that past. Most of the legends recounted here, including the Aeneas story, which belongs more to the world of myth than to that of legend, would have been regarded as historical by the Romans. Had you been a visitor to Rome in the first century BCE, say, any inhabitant you cared to ask would have pointed out to you the tree where the basket containing the twins Romulus and Remus washed up, the cave where the she-wolf later nurtured them, and the hut where the boys grew up under the care of their adoptive parents.

It's indisputable, however, that many of the legends in this book were invented or at least partly invented. Romulus, believed to have been the son of Mars, is clearly a mythical figure, though some present-day historians give credence to the deeds attributed to him. The life and deeds of the six kings who succeeded Romulus should also be treated with caution, though it seems likely that a period of kingship preceded the Republic, since an inscription found in the Forum contains the word *rex* or king, albeit followed by the limiting noun *sacrorum* in the genitive case, meaning 'in relation to sacred affairs'. Some 'aetiological' legends may have been invented to explain obscure customs or traditions. An example is Horatius Cocles' jump from the Sublician Bridge into the River Tiber, which recalls the tradition of throwing straw puppets from the bridge at a festival known as the Argei. Other 'etymological' legends may have grown up around a *cognomen*, a kind of nickname that was given to an individual which became hereditary. For instance, the name *Scaevola*, 'Left-handed', purportedly granted to a young man who sacrificed his right arm in the cause of duty, might originally have been a nickname assigned to a prominent one-armed man, whose descendants created the self-serving story to ennoble their family. Rome's second king Numa Pompilius might have acquired his reputation for religiosity solely because his name recalls the Latin noun *numen*, meaning 'divine power'. Rome's third king Tullus Hostilius might have been deemed bellicose solely because his name is cognate with the Latin adjective *hostilis*, meaning 'warlike'. Still other legends are exercises in wishful thinking, such as the report of the elderly patricians who calmly awaited the arrival of the Gauls dressed in their ceremonial robes. And so on.

There are places, too, where legends are at variance with what archaeology tells us. According to the tradition established in the first century BCE, Rome was founded in 753 – on 21 April to be precise, the day of the festival held in honour of a minor goddess called Pales, protector of shepherds. Archaeology, however, indicates that the future site of Rome was continuously occupied from at least as early as 1400 and that the earliest evidence for the existence of an organised centre, viz. the presence of something resembling a forum which was essential to its civic status, dates to about 650. This in turn raises the question whether Rome was ever 'founded' in one go, so to speak. Most ancient foundations are the product of steady growth and it is highly likely that Rome, too, wasn't built in a day. These problems aside, archaeology confirms that the ancient settlement did in fact expand in the mid-eighth century, in line with the traditional date of Rome's foundation.

I make no attempt to distinguish between legends that are historical, semi-historical, or downright fictitious. It's enough that the Romans thought a story worth preserving for the purposes of self-definition for it to be featured here. Moreover, I haven't hesitated to introduce my own variants for which there is no authority in our surviving accounts. Nowhere, for instance, do we read that King Latinus was abnormally short, nor that the future dictator Cincinnatus kept a senatorial delegation standing in the rain in a mud-soaked field while he took a leisurely shower. I include such vagaries in the interests of what I would like to call interest. In so doing I am merely following in the footsteps of the *maiores*, literally 'the greater ones', viz. the mighty dead, aka my ancient predecessors. Never once, however, do I wittingly compromise, debase or diminish the meaning that attaches to any legend in the form in which it has been preserved.

From the Oral to the Literary Tradition

Just like Greek myths, Roman legends were for many hundreds of years transmitted orally. Precisely what form oral transmission took is, however, a matter of debate. One influential theory is that the legends were performed as poetry at banquets, festivals, funerals and other social occasions. Whether or not this was the case, competing and often conflicting versions were certainly in circulation at the same time, as we see from discrepancies in our principal continuous sources for early Roman history, Livy and Dionysius of Halicarnassus. This circumstance, though it would be troubling to us, seems not to have bothered the Romans. Their historians saw it as their right to invent – or perhaps we should say more politely embellish – most obviously in regard to the *oratio recta* speeches which they inserted into their narratives.

No literary account of Rome's history of which we have knowledge predates the end of the third century. The man accounted the earliest historian is the aristocrat Fabius Pictor (flourished 200), who wrote a history in Greek from Rome's foundation to the middle of the third century. Only fragments of his work survive. The earliest historian to write in Latin was Cato the Censor (234–149), otherwise known as Cato the Elder. His work, called *Origins*, has likewise survived only in fragments. There also existed a body of state records compiled by the Chief Pontiff in the late second century known as the *Annales Maximi*. It contained a list of magistrates and references to public events that occurred in their year of office. It has not survived.

Our first extant histories of early Rome belong to the first centuries BCE and CE, that is to say, seven centuries after the legendary date of the city's foundation. The most valuable source for the legends that form the bulk of this work are the first five books of Livy's *History of Rome*, which deal with the foundation of Rome, the rule of the seven kings, the establishment of the Republic, Rome's many wars against her neighbours and her defeat of the Gauls. It originally comprised 142 books, of which only 35 survive as such; the remainder exist in summary form. Livy has his detractors, but I admire him enormously and we'd be utterly lost without him.

Livy (c. 59–CE 17) was living in the aftermath of a period of protracted civil war and the bitterness he felt towards his fellow countrymen entered into his account of Rome's early heroes. He regarded the study of history as an antidote to the ills of his own age. He also saw it as a way of instructing his readers in the virtues of duty and obedience, both civic and familial, and as a warning about the dangers of ambition and complacency. Duty and obedience, like piety, might not seem to amount to much these days, but it was precisely these virtues that made Rome great. And Rome, indisputably, was great. Unlike his predecessors and successors, Livy was not a politician, and being from Patavium (Padua) he was perhaps a provincial in more senses than one. The English word 'patavinity', derived from the Latin *patavinitas*, alludes to the charge levelled against Livy of writing in a style that displayed his provincial origin.

We also have Virgil's *Aeneid*, an epic poem in twelve books, which recounts the adventures of the Trojan prince Aeneas from his flight from Troy to his arrival in Italy. His story culminated, after many battles, in a union between Trojan refugees and the native Latin population. Virgil, another provincial (70–19), composed his poem at the bidding of the Emperor Augustus via a wealthy patron named Maecenas in order to justify the establishment in the 20s BCE of the new, post-Republican system of government called the Principate, which translates as 'rule by the *princeps* or first citizen'. This fact has coloured the *Aeneid*, which may be considered in part a reflection on the burdens of running an empire. Despite the fact that he was to some degree composing at the bidding of the emperor, Virgil makes it clear that he had serious reservations about Rome's rise to power and imperial grasp. I admit that Aeneas' adventures belong more to the realm of myth than they do to the world of legend, but sometimes there isn't a clear distinction between the two. Besides, many Romans, Livy among them, believed Aeneas, a

Trojan immigrant, to be their ancestor, which is why I have thought fit to include him in my narrative.

Dionysius of Halicarnassus (flourished 20), a Greek intellectual, wrote a romantic and somewhat sycophantic history of Rome from its foundation to the beginning of the First Punic War in 264 entitled *Roman Antiquities*, of which about the first half survives. Written in Greek, his history was intended to reconcile his Greek readers to Roman rule.

A Greek philosopher called Plutarch (c. CE 46–after 120) was the author of a compendium entitled *Parallel Lives of the Greeks and Romans*, which he wrote at the beginning of the second century CE. *Parallel Lives* comprises 23 pairs and four separate biographies, each pair consisting of a prominent Greek and a prominent Roman. It includes biographies of the two first kings of Rome, Romulus and Numa, and of many prominent figures in the Republic. Though his writing is not particularly profound, he distils his biographical accounts into a succession of dramatic gestures and memorable words with an emphasis upon the essence of his subjects' personality. Like Livy, Plutarch believed that history should be morally uplifting, and he was at pains to emphasise how character shaped destiny, both individual and collective.

There are other sources for early Roman history, but these are the main ones, and when we reach the first century they multiply enormously, not least due to the voluminous correspondence of the celebrated orator and politician Marcus Tullius Cicero (106–43), whose hundreds of preserved letters provide invaluable testimony regarding Caesar's dwindling popularity at the end of his life.

The Foundation of Rome

The Aeneas story presents a particular problem. The hero first appears in Homer's *Iliad* as a Trojan hero who is rescued from the battlefield by the sea god Poseidon (Roman Neptune). Poseidon prophesies to him that he and his descendants will one day be kings, but he does not indicate where their kingdom will be. Aeneas' first association with Rome comes through a Greek historian called Hellanicus from the island of Lesbos, who lived in the fifth century. Hellanicus makes Aeneas the founder of Rome, which he called Rhome after one of the women who accompanied him from Troy. (It's worth pointing out that 'Rhome' in Greek could mean 'strength'.) Another Greek version of Rome's foundation maintained that Rome was founded by a son of Odysseus and the witch Circe.

In addition to these Greek accounts, the Romans had a homegrown version of their city's foundation by the twins, Romulus and Remus. Even so, the Aeneas story had much to commend it because it enabled them to trace their origins back to the era of the Trojan War and thus claim an antiquity more nearly equal to that of the Greeks. The legend also explained the animosity that existed between the Romans and the Greeks, to which Virgil himself was not immune, as we see from his portrayal of the trickster Sinon in his description of the fall of Troy.

An obvious way to accommodate both the Greek and the Roman versions was by making Romulus and Remus descendants of Aeneas. However, when a Greek scholar called Eratosthenes of Cyrene, who lived in the third century, proposed that Troy fell in what we call 1184, a yawning gap of several hundred years emerged between the two traditions. Probably towards the end of the third century the Romans solved this dilemma by claiming that Aeneas had founded not Rome but a city in Latium called Lavinium and that his son Ascanius had founded another city in Latium called Alba Longa. Ascanius was succeeded as king of Alba Longa by a son or brother called Silvius. Silvius was the first in a line of obscure Alban kings, who conveniently filled the gap of centuries before Romulus and Remus, the 'actual' founders of Rome, were born.

The Role of the Supernatural

Though the gods don't play a central role in Roman legends, they are often there in the background, and it's important to bear in mind that the Romans were a deeply religious people. Even a highly sophisticated thinker like Cicero didn't deny the existence of the gods. The Romans believe that human existence is subject to a multiplicity of divine forces that are constantly warring against one another. The gods who embody these forces incorporate both good and evil. They have little invested in functioning as upholders of morality, unless it involves their self-interest.

Like the Greeks, from whom they borrowed so much, the Romans believed their gods to be anthropomorphic – human in shape and with human attributes, human desires, and human defects: superhuman physically but subhuman morally. Archaeological evidence suggests that as early as the sixth century the Romans had begun to identify their own gods with their Greek equivalents. Zeus became assimilated to Roman Jupiter, an amalgam of the words 'Zeus' and *'pater'*, meaning 'father Zeus'; Hera, his wife, became assimilated to Roman Juno; Aphrodite, goddess of love and beauty, to Venus; Athena, goddess of women's crafts, to Minerva; Ares, god of war, to Mars; Hermes, the messenger god, to Mercury; Hephaestus, god of fire and metalwork, to Vulcan, and so on. In the course of this process, some Roman deities acquired a greater importance than they had possessed previously in keeping with their Greek equivalents. Neptune, for instance, was in origin a river god who, by assimilation to Poseidon, was promoted to the rank of god of the sea.

Deities were worshipped *en plein air* chiefly by means of sacrifices performed in their honour. Temples erected to gods were supervised by priests; those erected to goddesses by priestesses. An important part in the narrative is played by the Vestal Virgins, who devoted their lives to the service of Vesta, goddess of the hearth. It was their job to ensure that the sacred flame inside her temple remained perpetually alight. If it were to be extinguished, Rome would be placed in mortal peril. If a Vestal broke her vow of chastity, she was scourged, beaten and buried alive. On many occasions, we may suspect, one or more Vestals were unjustly punished when a catastrophe struck. Vestal Virgins were placed under the authority of the *pontifex maximus* or Chief Pontiff, the head of Rome's religious establishment. According to legend, Rome's foundation derived from the rape of a Vestal Virgin – an action freighted with symbolism.

A prominent feature in a number of legends is the belief that gods communicated with humans through signs. Typical signs include the flight of birds, especially that of eagles and vultures; the health or otherwise of the entrails of a sacrificial animal; and meteorological phenomena such as lightning. Sometimes the gods sent coded messages via a medium, who acted as an interpreter of their oracular utterances. Oracular utterances were also preserved in ancient writings. It was vital to take the auspices, as the ritual of consulting the gods was called, before going to war. The foremost god of prophecy is Apollo, whose most important shrine was located at Delphi in central Greece. Apollo also had an important shrine at Cumae on the west coast of Italy, which Aeneas visited.

Though gods didn't expect their worshippers to display the qualities of obedience, love, humility, mercy, and so on that are associated with most religious systems we are familiar with, a quintessential virtue which they did expect from them is *pietas*, from which our somewhat watered-down word 'piety' derives. *Pietas* is intimately associated with Aeneas, who introduces himself with the words, *sum pius Aeneas,* 'I am pious Aeneas'. He exhibited *pietas* to the gods, to his father, and to the dead. It is an attribute without any modern equivalent of equal force.

And talking of the dead, they, too, are a powerful presence in the lives of their descendants. Their worship takes a variety of forms. As the *lemures* they are the troublesome dead, as the *maiores*, literal translation 'the greater ones', they are the dead in general, and as the *dii manes* they are the deified dead. The multiplicity of their identities signals their centrality. The *mos maiorum*, an almost untranslatable concept that means something akin to 'traditional practice as established by the dead', acted as an important incentive and check in both public and private life, though immemorial 'custom' or 'tradition' might in some cases have been invented quite recently. The esteem in which the Romans held their ancestors contributed to the value they invested in the legends attached to their city's foundation and growth.

In addition to gods and the dead, there was also an impersonal agent, fate or the fates – which so arranged matters that the Romans were destined to rule other peoples. The fates make an important appearance in the Preface to Livy's *History* where he writes, 'The foundation of so great a city and the beginning of the most powerful empire, second only to that of the gods, was in my view owed to (i.e. determined by) the fates.' Another way of saying this would be, 'It certainly wasn't a foregone conclusion that Rome would come to dominate the Mediterranean', and his following account gives us a striking picture of a state that is riven by internal discord and constantly having to fight off its neighbours to survive.

I'm with Livy. The fates must have had something to do with it.

An Average Roman Summarises His City's History

There's no obvious place to end a book on Roman legends because there's no definitive moment when legend is replaced by fact. The period of history which this book covers begins with the destruction of

Troy – assuming the Trojan War is a historical event, though a siege lasting 10 years is undoubtedly a fiction – in c. 1150 (Eratosthenes wasn't far off the mark) and ends with the assassination of Julius Caesar in 44. By concluding in the dying years of the Republic and giving the kiss of death (literally) to Julius Caesar, who traced his descent back to Venus Genetrix, 'the Mother', the ancestral mother of Aeneas, I bestow upon my work a pleasing if superficial circularity. Besides which, what is not legendary about Spartacus, Sulla, Brutus, Caesar and Cleopatra – all of whom are larger than life?

Here is how an average Roman living at the turn of the Common Era might have summarised this 710-year period of history:

'For the first 250 years of its existence, my city was ruled by kings, the first of whom was Romulus, its founder. When his brother Remus mocked its walls, Romulus killed him in a fit of rage. Good riddance. To begin with, my ancestors struggled to reproduce themselves, so much so that Romulus allowed the basest elements to seek asylum in the city. When there weren't enough women to go around, he abducted a number of them from a neighbouring people called the Sabines. Throughout the regal period Rome was beset on all sides by numerous foes. It only survived thanks to the willingness of the few to sacrifice themselves to the common good. It was also greatly to our advantage that my ancestors were hospitable to foreigners. Two of our kings were actually foreigners.

'Our first six kings were fairly benign, at least in terms of the exercise of their royal power. Our last king, however, aptly named Tarquin the Proud because of his tyrannical nature, had a son called Sextus, who raped a woman called Lucretia. By this point my ancestors had had enough of kings, so they kicked him out. Good riddance. A nobleman called Lucius Junius Brutus established a system of government known as a republic. *Respublica* means that everything is held in common. Our republic consists of two elements – an advisory body known as the Senate and everybody else, including me, known collectively as the plebs. To prevent any individual from amassing power, a slew of magistrates is elected, whose term of office lasts only one year. The two chief magistrates are the consuls, who have the power to veto each other's proposals. Each consul also commands two legions. Next most important are the praetors, in overall charge of lawsuits.

'Long ago the office of the tribunate of the plebs was established to safeguard the rights of poor people like myself against members of the higher class known as patricians. Harmony, however, did not prevail and there were frequent clashes between the Senate and the plebs, notably in the time of Coriolanus, a highly decorated military commander, who held us in abject contempt. Ambition got the better of him, however, as it has done for many of our most successful generals and politicians, and when the tribunes admonished him for his insolence, he deserted Rome and sided with our enemies. Good riddance. My personal hero is Cincinnatus, who was appointed dictator and who having won a resounding victory, immediately resigned. An even more deadly threat was posed by the Gauls, who burned our city to the ground. Afterwards, my ancestors wanted to abandon Rome but a general called Camillus persuaded them to stay. Camillus is revered as our second founder.

'Gradually my ancestors came to dominate the Italian peninsula. Then a Carthaginian called Hannibal crossed the spinal Alps and destroyed almost all of our fighting capacity by his tactical superiority. We didn't give in, however, and eventually he gave up. Two generations later we wiped Carthage off the face of the earth. Absolute good riddance. Lots more happened, including our conquest of what remained from the original empire of Alexander the Great. This resulted in an influx of educated Greek slaves, as a result of which we became better educated and more sophisticated. Not that I care for the Greeks, a slimy and supercilious bunch who look down their noses at us. Things started to fall apart in the first period of civil war in the time of Marius and Sulla, Marius being the general who made our army professional. Then Julius Caesar tore up the rule book after subjugating the whole of Gaul by initiating an even bigger civil war between him and his rival (and son-in-law) Pompey the Great, which Caesar won. After his victory, he pardoned all his enemies. Big mistake. Such was the hatred he had incurred that a conspiracy of eighty senators was formed under the leadership of Marcus Brutus and Gaius Cassius. Marcus Brutus was a descendant of Lucius Brutus, the man who established the Republic. Caesar was assassinated on what we commemorate as Patricide Day, the infamous Ides of March. It's so called because he was father of the fatherland. His murder was the worst crime in history.

'What follows isn't in this book but here goes. Caesar's assassination ushered in another period of civil war, between a delinquent drunk called Mark Antony, who deserted his country for his Egyptian whore

Cleopatra, and Octavian, Caesar's grandnephew and adopted heir. After being defeated by Octavian's lieutenant Agrippa at sea, they both committed suicide. Good riddance. Octavian, who henceforth called himself Augustus, which means 'Revered one', restored the Republic, or so he claimed, and established the Principate. The Principate is a jolly good thing, if you ask me, and there haven't been any civil wars since. And through all this turmoil, our city has prospered and grown, like no other city in the world.'

Why the Legends Were – and Are – Important to This Day

As we've just seen from the perspective of our average Roman, the city's rise wasn't meteoric. Far from it. Nor was it inevitable. One of the boldest, most enduring, and most successful political experiments in human history begins with defeat, despair and failure. A desperate band of refugees escaped from the ruins of a burning city and, after taking many wrong turns and undergoing much hardship, established itself in the land of Hesperia, the Western Land, aka Italia. Warlike valour played its part in this achievement, but so did political compromise and a willingness to give up the name of one's ancestors by intermarrying with the local population. It was in this way that a mixed race came to dominate first its immediate neighbourhood, then its region, next peninsular Italy, and finally the Mediterranean and beyond. There's a lesson there somewhere.

The Romans understand all too well that being an imperial power carries a heavy price tag, not only for the conquered but also for the conqueror, and they do not seek to disguise that fact from themselves. Rome's foundation isn't an uplifting tale of human progress. Social and political change is slow and halting. Almost all the characters we will encounter are seriously flawed; some are despicable. Terrible crimes, including rape, attempted infanticide and fratricide, play their part in the story. The fact, however, that these legends record unsparingly the dark side of Rome's destiny is what makes them so memorable and so insightful. What the Romans are saying to themselves and to us, their cultural descendants, is, unflinchingly, 'This is the unvarnished truth. This is who we are.'

It follows that these stories are important not only because they preserve some memory of Roman history, but also because they remind the Romans who they (think they) are as a people, how humble and inauspicious were their beginnings, and how distinctive was the character of the men and women who shaped their destiny. By repeatedly insisting upon the need to put one's country before one's family and one's duty before one's personal ambitions, they tell us a lot about how a people sees itself.

When Aeneas visits the Underworld in *Aeneid* Book 6, the shade of his father Anchises articulates the Romans' mission statement. He tells him their role will be 'to spare the subjected and render the proud unwarlike' (literally 'war down the proud'). It's easy to point out the many instances where the Romans failed to live up to this lofty aim, but, like the legends, this too tells us a lot about how the Romans saw themselves, as well as how they saw their subjects as subjects.

It is not my purpose to whitewash the Romans, who had an inordinate propensity for inflicting cruelty on anyone who stood in the way of their rise to power. Hundreds of thousands of slaves were worked to death in conditions of unimaginable squalor. Hundreds of thousands of prisoners were slaughtered in cold blood. Poverty was widespread and rampant. Social inequalities were vast. But at the risk of being charged with condoning their inhumanity, as well as their many failures and shortcomings, I half-heartedly salute the Romans for establishing peace ('they make a desert and call it "peace"' as the historian Tacitus pointed out) over such a vast area – well over five and a half million square miles at their empire's greatest extent and with a population of about fifty million at a conservative estimate – and I commend them for accommodating, mostly peaceably, so many different peoples under a single system of government.

Chapter 1

Aeneas' Escape From Troy

Let's not make any bones about it. Rome's ancestors, the Trojans, were losers. Their city was destroyed by the Mycenaean Greeks after a siege that had allegedly lasted ten years. They're called the Mycenaean Greeks because their leading city was Mycenae, a fortress with massive walls situated in the northeast Peloponnese, southern Greece – so massive that they were thought in later times to have been constructed by the giant one-eyed Cyclopes, sons of Poseidon, lord of the watery paths. The Trojans lost not because they were inferior fighters but because of a ruse that was practised upon them by the canny Greeks – the famous ruse of the wooden horse. That was one reason. The other reason for Troy's ruin was the implacable enmity of some of the gods. No enmity is more implacable than that which is divine.

Here's the backstory. The Greeks, under their commander-in-chief Agamemnon, lord of Mycenae, launched a vast naval expedition against Troy to recover Helen, the wife of Agamemnon's brother Menelaus, lord of Sparta. Helen had been either abducted or seduced – choose which word you prefer – by a prince of the Trojan royal house called Paris, son of Priam. This led to the launch of a fleet of well over 1,000 ships, to which communities of Greeks contributed from all over the Mycenaean-dominated world, out of fealty to Agamemnon.

One of the greatest heroes on the Trojan side was a warrior called Aeneas. Aeneas was the son of Venus, the Greek goddess of love and beauty, and Anchises, a minor Trojan royal. It's with Aeneas that Rome's story begins.

After ten years of fighting, the siege of Troy had reached a stalemate, so Ulysses – his Greek name was Odysseus – came up with the idea of taking Troy by subterfuge.

'Here's my brilliant plan', he said in an assembly of the soldiery in the tenth year of the siege when everyone was on the verge of giving up. 'I suggest we construct a wooden horse with a hollow belly, fill it with a contingent of men, and leave it outside the city as a kind of present or peace offering. Then we burn our tents, board our ships and sail away

HELEN of TROY

Helen of Troy.

into the sunset. This'll give the appearance that we've given up hope of ever taking Troy and gone home. Except we won't be sailing away into the sunset. We'll hide our ships on an island and return the next day. Meanwhile the men concealed inside the horse will secretly open the gates to let the rest of the army in and we'll take the Trojans by storm. It'll be a bloodbath.'

'It's certainly worth a shot', Agamemnon said begrudgingly, wishing that he'd thought of the plan first and rather sooner. 'All those in favour say aye.'

'Aye!' all the Greeks shouted, ready to endorse any plan that offered some hope of ending the war.

The wooden horse.

When saffron-robed dawn spread over the earth next morning, the Trojans were amazed to discover that the shore was deserted but for a huddle of smouldering tents and a colossal wooden horse. King Priam, too, held an assembly. This was a feature of warfare in those far off heroic times. Decisions were put before the soldiers for ratification. The one item under discussion was whether to destroy the horse or take it inside their city.

The leading proponent of the destroy-the-horse-at-all-costs faction was Laocoön, a priest of Neptune/Poseidon. Laocoön was convinced that the horse was a trick. He even went so far as to throw his spear at its hollow belly, thereby causing the armour that the men were wearing inside to clatter as they banged into each other. You'd think the Trojans would have smelled a rat at this juncture, but as fate would have it just then some shepherds appeared, dragging along a dishevelled Greek with furry eyebrows, braided locks and a long beard.

The fellow, whose name was Sinon, claimed that his compatriots had intended to kill him for having insulted Ulysses. He'd managed to escape by hiding in a ditch, and in the end they'd sailed off without him.

3

'I hate Ulysses, hate Agamemnon, and hate all Greeks! Damn the lot of them', Sinon truculently declared.

So saying, he produced a large gob of spit and spat on the ground.

Naturally they asked him about the wooden horse.

'The horse? Oh, that's intended as a gift to silver-footed Minerva/Athena', Sinon told them offhandedly. 'Haven't you worked that out? The Greeks want Minerva's help to get back safely to Greece. They're afraid she'll connive with Neptune to cause a storm and wreck their fleet. If you bring the horse inside your city, it'll function as a protective talisman instead. That means Agamemnon will be screwed. On the other hand, if you destroy it, you'll bring the wrath of Minerva down on your heads.'

'But the horse is too big to fit through the gates', piped up Dolops, a very minor Trojan hero. 'We'd have to demolish part of the city wall.'

'Duh. That's the whole point', Sinon explained contemptuously. 'The Greeks don't *want* you to take the horse inside. That's why they made it so big. I swear by all the gods what I've told you is true. I know what I'd do. Still, it's up to you to decide what's in your best interests.'

When he finished speaking, the anti-horsers and the pro-horsers were pretty much evenly divided. Priam was about to call a vote when two monstrous and slimy snakes emerged from the sea. Their tongues flicking, the snakes slunk at speed along the shore towards Laocoön and his two sons. Before they had time to react, the reptiles were encircling their ankles. Soon they had coiled around their bodies and the eyes of all three were literally popping out of their heads. The Trojans were horrified. That settled matters. Everyone assumed that Laocoön had offended the gods by throwing his spear at what was intended as a gift. Without further ado Priam ordered the Trojans to attach wheels to the legs of the wooden horse and to haul it up from the shore. They had to destroy the lintel over the main gates to accommodate it inside the city.

Only princess Cassandra, Priam's daughter, knew it was a trick. She tried to warn them that ruin would follow if they took the horse inside, but no one believed her. No one *ever* believed her. Cassandra had promised to sleep with Apollo if he gave her the gift of prophecy. Once she'd received his gift, however, she broke her promise. Apollo couldn't break *his* word – gods can never take their gifts back – so by way of punishment he decreed that no one would ever believe her prophecies. Hers was a fate worse than death: to foresee disaster and be powerless to avert it.

4

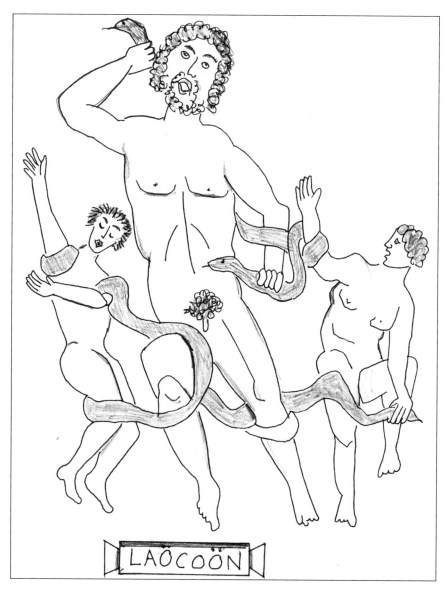

Laocoön.

That night the Trojans partied big time. The Greeks had departed, the siege was lifted, and to cap it all, they had the protection of the gods. Game over. Finally, they could relax.

But not so fast. Nothing is as simple as it seems, especially when it comes to dealings with the Greeks, the trickiest race on the face of the earth, so the Romans believed. This is where the phrase, 'I fear Greeks *especially* (or *even*) when they're bringing gifts' comes from. But the Trojans had yet to learn the meaning of the phrase, which Virgil coined.

Because, as we know, the Greeks hadn't sailed home. They'd sailed to an island called Tenedos, way out of sight of the Trojans. And while the Trojans were partying, the Greeks inside the wooden horse opened a concealed door under its belly, let down a rope ladder and gingerly climbed down. Then they tiptoed to the main gates and threw back the horizontal bar that kept them secured. Everyone was fast asleep, there weren't any guards on duty, and they entered completely unobserved.

As soon as they received a signal from inside the city, they disembarked and ran to the city. What followed was a bloodbath, as Ulysses had predicted. All the children and old men were butchered. All the women were bound over as sex slaves.

The gods were at least as guilty as the Greeks. That's because the ultimate origin of the Trojan War was the contest for a golden apple that the goddess Eris or Contention had tossed among the guests at the wedding of Peleus, the future father of Achilles, and a sea deity called Thetis. Eris was angry at having been excluded from the guest list – why would you invite Contention to a wedding? – and she determined to get even by breaking the party up. Inscribed on the golden apple were the words, 'For the fairest woman'. She intended to set the proverbial cat among the pigeons. Which goddess who possessed an ounce of dignity, not to mention pride, wouldn't claim for herself that coveted title?

Eventually the field got narrowed down to three goddesses: Juno, wife of Jupiter, Minerva, Jupiter's daughter, and Venus, goddess of beauty. But who could the contestants find to be an impartial judge? Certainly not any of the gods. They were all corrupt. After much deliberation, the three agreed to submit to the judgement of a humble Trojan shepherd boy called Paris.

But Paris turned out to be just as bent as the gods were. Each of the three goddesses offered him a bribe. Juno offered him wealth and power, Minerva offered him victory in war, and Venus offered him the most beautiful woman in the world. He chose the most beautiful woman in the world and gave the prize to Venus. It just so happened, however, that the most beautiful woman in the world was married to Agamemnon's brother Menelaus, king of Sparta. Big problemo.

Juno and Minerva were incensed at being passed over. That is why the goddesses joined the Greek side and that is why, at this moment, they were helping the Greeks to destroy Troy.

There's no limit to what the gods and goddesses will do to you if you ruffle their feathers. They're vengeful, unpredictable and violent. Well, that's stereotyping, I admit. It's true that Venus cared for her son Aeneas, even if she didn't always do a good job in protecting him. And it's true as well that Jupiter had an eye for the bigger picture, by which I mean he had the good of the Roman race in mind, even if he lost the plot at times.

While heady murder, spoil and villainy, to quote Shakespeare, gripped Troy, Aeneas, who was one of the few Trojan warriors who wasn't blind drunk, strapped on his bronze corselet and greaves, donned his shining helmet, picked up his weighty shield, grabbed his steely bronze sword, and rushed headlong into the fray. He soon realised that it was a lost cause. There was no way Troy could be saved at this point. The city was falling into ruin. 'Troy had been', as Virgil memorably put it.

Aeneas was about to return to his family when he caught sight of Helen, the cause of all the destruction.

'At least I can achieve a symbolic victory by killing her', he said to himself. 'That's something.'

He raised his spear, took careful aim, and was about to let fly when Venus appeared, enveloped in a ghostly haze.

'Leave her alone!' the goddess commanded sternly. 'She's not to blame for what's happening. Troy is being destroyed because the gods hate it.'

Aeneas lowered his spear. Suddenly all his thoughts were directed towards the safety of his precocious son Ascanius, his elderly father Anchises, and his placid wife Creusa, alone and at the mercy of the Greeks. He raced back home.

'We have to leave immediately!' he expostulated, bursting through the door. 'There's no time to pack. Just grab the household gods. That's all we're taking.'

A word about household gods. Every Roman family has its own set, to whom it prays and sacrifices every morning. Household gods keep the wolf from the door by ensuring that there is enough food in the larder. They generally reside in the kitchen inside a portable shrine resembling a small cabinet some eighteen inches in height. The head of the household, the so-called *paterfamilias*, brings them out at mealtimes, places them

7

on the table where his family is eating, and gives them a portion of the meal. The set that Aeneas possessed resembled a miniature temple with a pediment and columns made out of terracotta. Inside were two bronze statuettes of young men.

'It's your job to look after these guys', Aeneas said to his father, after reverently receiving the shrine from Creusa. 'We're going to need them when we settle somewhere new. They represent the continuity of our family, as we all know.'

'I'm not going anywhere', Anchises announced petulantly, pushing the shrine away and sitting down at the hearth. 'I'm an old man and I'd only be a burden to you at this point. You're much better off without me. I've lived in Troy all my life and I intend to die here. Added to which, my bloody feet are killing me. How do you think I could possibly keep up with you?'

'But the Greeks will hack you to pieces!' Aeneas protested violently. 'I can't leave you behind. How could I possibly live with myself? It would be an act of impiety. You're my father. It's my duty to protect you. And you won't have to walk. I'll carry you.'

'Abandoning me isn't an act of impiety because I'm not giving you any choice, son', Anchises replied. 'On the contrary, it would be an act of impiety to overrule me. Now leave.'

'Why are you always so confoundedly obstinate, controlling, self-righteous, judgmental, opinionated, self-dramatising, and – and – inflammatory?' Aeneas demanded exasperatedly. 'Our welfare depends on you. Can't you think of someone other than yourself for once in your life? No wonder my divine mother left you. I bet you drove her up the wall.'

Before the old man had a chance to respond, a giant ball of fire appeared out of nowhere and began wrapping Ascanius' head in flames. What was truly amazing, however, was the fact that the boy himself remained unharmed. Indeed, he seemed completely unaware.

'That's obviously a sign from Jupiter the cloud-gatherer', Aeneas observed flatly. 'He's had enough of your shillyshallying. He's ordering you out of here double quick. Now will you do what I say?'

'Hmm, not so fast', Anchises replied. 'Not so fast. Maybe the flames are just a freak of nature. It's never good to jump to conclusions.'

'A freak of nature?' Aeneas repeated incredulously, throwing his arms up in despair. 'Are you out of your tiny mind? Don't you know a sign from Jupiter when you see one? How many times have you seen flames enveloping a boy's head without singeing his hair?'

'Well, I say it's a freak of nature and if Jupiter wants me to abandon Troy, he'd jolly well better send me another sign', Anchises said equally flatly, crossing his arms defiantly. 'Otherwise, I'm staying put.'

As if on cue, a blinding flash of lightning lit up the sky, visible through the open door. This was followed by an ear-piercing clap of thunder that caused all the furniture to rattle.

'OK, OK', Anchises said, hastily rising and grabbing his hat and cloak from a peg. 'I got the message. I'm coming with you.'

Once outside, Aeneas knelt down so that his father could climb onto his shoulders. The old man weighed next to nothing. Then Creusa handed Anchises the household gods, which he cradled in his arms. Aeneas grabbed Ascanius by his right hand and clenched it tightly. The little family made its way by a circuitous route to a postern gate, Creusa keeping up the rear. More than once they had to step over piles of corpses that lay across their path.

A full moon lit their path as they headed inland towards Mount Ida, which long ago Priam had arranged to be the rendezvous point for survivors, if Troy should ever fall to the Greeks.

Aeneas sensed danger every step of the way. At times he increased his speed to a trot, fearing that they were being pursued. All the while Ascanius tried to match his little steps to his father's. When they came to a secluded copse of cypress trees that offered protection from the path they were on, Aeneas decided to take a breather. He crouched down so that Anchises could slide off his back. Then he patted Ascanius on the shoulder.

'Good job, son', he said. Then, turning around, he asked, 'Where's your mother?'

'I don't know. I never looked back', Ascanius replied.

Frantically they both scoured the path they had taken. Creusa was nowhere to be seen.

'Mummy!' Ascanius cried out frantically. 'Mummy, where are you?' There was no reply.

'Wait here both of you', Aeneas ordered. 'I'll be back soon.'

Aeneas rapidly retraced his steps, scanning the terrain on both sides of the path. The journey back was easy because the orange glow of the burning city guided him. By the time he reached the outskirts of Troy,

Aeneas escapes with his family from Troy.

flames were engulfing the city in every quarter. He muffled his mouth with his tunic and narrowly escaped being struck by the column of a temple that crashed to the ground only a few inches in front of him. He was cautiously picking his way between lumps of smashed stone and charred wood when the ghost of Creusa appeared in front of him.

The sight of her caused the hair on the back of his neck to stand on end.

'Search for me no longer, dear husband', the misty spectre said. 'It is not written in the book of fate for me to accompany you on your journey. I do not belong to your future. Many trials lie ahead but eventually your wanderings will cease. A place called Latium will become your new home in a country called Hesperia. There you will marry a princess and become the founder of a mixed race. Such is the will of Jupiter. Goodbye, Aeneas. Remember me from time to time.'

Aeneas stepped towards her and tried to embrace her, not once but three times. Each time, however, he found himself grasping at metaphorical straws.

'Don't leave me!' he cried. 'How can I go on without you? I need you, Creusa!'

The spectre dissolved without saying another word. There was nothing he could do. Brushing away his tears, he turned around and began to head back with heavy steps to the copse where he had left Anchises and Ascanius.

'Well?' Ascanius asked as soon as he detected the dark form of his father emerging from the gloom. 'Where's mummy?'

'She's been detained', Aeneas replied, kneeling down and tenderly hugging his son. 'She told me we must go on without her. She's safe. No harm can come to her now.'

'How can she be safe if she's still in Troy?' Ascanius demanded, fighting back his tears.

'It's complicated. We must trust in the will of Jupiter. That's what she told me. Everything that's happening is in accordance with his will. There's no time for tears. We have to go on our way.'

'But you saw her?'

'Yes, I did. Just as I see you now.'

'And you talked to her.'

'I did.'

'And she was well?'

'Yes, she's well. The gods are looking after her. She's in their good hands.'

Aeneas lifted Anchises back onto his shoulders, grabbed Ascanius by the hand, and they continued on their way. None of them said a word. Once they arrived at the foothills of Mount Ida, Aeneas and his family were greeted by hundreds of refugees. Finding a sheltered nook, they were lulled to sleep by a hoarse chorus of tree frogs.

Under Aeneas' leadership the refugees spent the next month shipbuilding – cutting down pine trees, fashioning keels and ribs, inserting deck beams, caulking all the joints and cracks in the wood, and sewing sail cloth, to which they added cringles, eyelets and grommets. Once all was ready, they sacrificed a hundred oxen to Neptune, the protector from earthquakes, launched their beaked ships into the loud-sounding sea, and set sail in search of the enigmatic land of Hesperia.

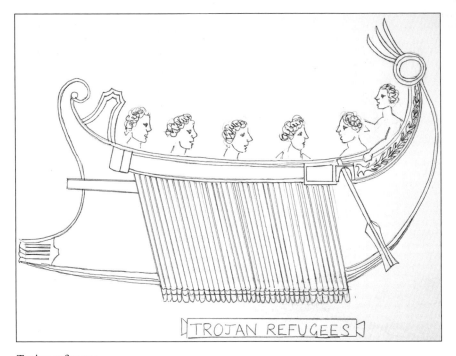

Trojan refugees.

Chapter 2

Dido, Queen of Carthage

It seemed as if all the planets had aligned. On the one hand, we have Aeneas, a widower, a valiant warrior of considerable renown, the leader of a band of refugees, the father of a young son, in search of a place to put down roots; on the other hand, we have Dido, a childless widow, the leader of an erstwhile band of refugees, establishing a new city at Carthage in what the Romans call Libya (modern-day Tunisia). If that wasn't a match made in heaven, what is?

Years passed. The seasons turned. It was again winter. Aeneas and his men continued cruising around the Mediterranean – *mare nostrum*, 'our sea', as the Romans would one day provincially call it – looking for Hesperia and a place to found a settlement. Well, cruising isn't perhaps the right word, given the challenges of the weather, but you get the general picture. After a number of adventures, too tedious to mention, and after many near-death brushes with inanition, they landed in Sicily, where old Anchises finally breathed his last.

Aeneas stroked the few remaining strands of his father's hair and kissed his ivory forehead.

'Goodbye, best of dads', he said, sobbing piteously. 'I'm very sorry for all the nasty things I said about you when I was trying to get you to leave Troy.'

Then he hurled a firebrand onto the pyre and watched as the smoke curled upwards.

Once the pyre had burnt itself out, he gathered his father's ashes into an urn, which he buried under a heaped-up mound. Again they set sail, trusting that providence would guide them. Before long, however, the sky became lead grey, a gale arose, and the waves started to crest before plunging into the dark depths below. The timbers of Aeneas' ship creaked ominously and the cargo below shifted back and forth from wall to wall. This was no freak storm, however. Like so many events in this world, it was the work of the gods – in this case the work of Juno.

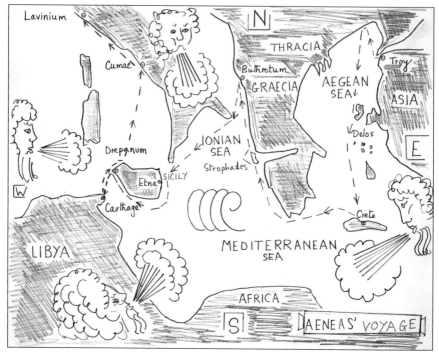

Aeneas' travels.

Juno, as we've seen, hated the Trojans with passionate intensity because of Paris, the Trojan prince who had given the golden apple to Venus. With sublime illogicality, she hated all Trojans indiscriminately. Only if she could devour all the Trojans raw might she have assuaged her wrath, as Jupiter had sardonically suggested.

There was another reason for her enmity. She'd heard that a race descended from the Trojans would one day destroy Carthage, a city she loved because of the devotion of its people. Forget the fact that Jupiter had singled out Aeneas to be the patriarch of this new race and that she was powerless to oppose his will. She was determined to wreak as much havoc as she could. You'd think that the gods would be incapable of such senseless anger. Well, you'd be wrong.

As soon as Aeneas set sail, cloudlets appeared high above the horizon. Then a north wind, followed by a south wind, followed by an east wind scattered his fleet to the three winds. Juno had bribed Aeolus, the keeper of the winds, to release them from their underwater cage. As in the human world so in the divine, no one does anything for nothing.

14

Juno.

Same old, same old. Juno had bribed him with the offer of a beautiful nymph. The guy was only a minor factotum, however. He answered to his boss Neptune, the Earthshaker, and when Neptune found out the havoc that his underling had caused, he literally went ballistic.

'How dare you go on a rampage without my bidding!' he roared at the winds as they swirled around his head. 'Tell your master that it's me who wields the trident – not him.'

Saying which, the god leapt into his barnacle-encrusted chariot drawn by two white prancing sea horses, cracked his whip, and instantly calmed the sea lanes so that they were safe for shipping once more.

The Earthshaker had intervened just in time. Aeneas' ship had been on the point of breaking up when suddenly the squall died. Shortly afterwards his helmsman Palinurus spied land and guided their ship

Neptune calms the tempest.

16

into a sheltered inlet. It ended in a cave with seats cut into the rock to accommodate the fifty oceanids, the submersible daughters of the Titan Oceanus. The men furled the sails and stowed them in the hold. Then they lowered the masts by means of the forestays and laid them horizontally on the decks. Then they fell asleep.

Aeneas rose well before Phoebus had bathed the earth in his golden rays. Accompanied by his closest companion, a dour and rather tight-lipped fellow called Achates, he went on a scouting expedition. As soon as they had climbed up onto a rocky eminence to get a view of the land, they espied a herd of deer grazing in a meadow. Aeneas took aim with his bow and shot seven deer in quick succession, one for each of his seven ships that had managed to survive the storm. On returning to the inlet, he sent a handful of men to drag back the deer, which they later roasted on makeshift spits.

While they were still greedily licking their sticky fingers, Aeneas gave a rousing address.

'Look here, fellow Trojans', he began, smacking a mosquito that had settled on his neck. 'When you think about it, things could be a lot worse. We might all have been drowned for starters. But we weren't. We survived. We're the lucky ones. Think about all the dangers we've overcome. Remember Scylla and Charybdis? Scylla was that hideous barking creature with a belt of dogs around her waist, which devoured lots of our mates. Charybdis was that whirlpool which sucked our ships down into its unfathomable depths. It's a bloody miracle we're here to tell the tale, if you ask me. One day, when we settle in Hesperia, you're going to take pleasure in telling the tale of our adventures to your grandchildren, I promise you. A god has had a hand in preserving us. Stuff like this doesn't happen without divine intervention. So, some gratitude to the powers that be is in order. And by the way – did I tell you this? – I can't remember – I've had a lot on my mind of late – we're going to become the founders of a new race. Posterity will celebrate our daring. Everything will turn out well in the end. It always does.'

Aeneas was only faking it, of course. He didn't believe any of this. He was actually feeling extremely depressed – so much so that he found himself wishing that he had died fighting at Troy. But he knew it was his job to chivy his men, so he wasn't about to tell them that the logical thing to do was to give up hope. 'While I breathe, I hope', as the Roman saying goes. Or, in the laconic Latin, '*Dum spiro, spero.*'

Aeneas was certainly right about one thing. The gods were in on the mix. While he and his men were recovering from the tempest, Jupiter sent his messenger Mercury, the god with the wingèd sandals and wingèd hat, all the way down from Mount Olympus, where the blessed ones reside, to Carthage, which happened to be within walking distance of where Aeneas and his men had landed.

Jupiter had instructed Mercury to make Dido and her people hospitable to the Trojans. I should perhaps explain that gods don't only control the elements. They also mess with the insides of people's heads by creating mood swings, driving them hysterical, or permanently changing their mindset. They can also make them fall hopelessly in love.

After giving his little pep talk, Aeneas told his men to stay beside their ships, while he, accompanied again by the taciturn Achates, went off to explore the local neighbourhood. They hadn't gone far when they espied an attractive young woman in hunting gear, viz. leather jerkin with shiny bronze studs, matching short leather skirt, and thigh-length leather boots. She was grasping a bow in her right hand and had a quiver full of arrows slung over her left shoulder.

'Good morning, miss', Aeneas said to her, politely tipping his broad-brimmed traveller's hat, which he'd somehow managed to salvage from the storm. 'Could you tell me where I am? I'm new to these parts. My ship narrowly escaped destruction last night.'

'By all means, handsome stranger', the huntress – actually Aeneas' mother, Venus, in disguise – coyly replied. 'You're on the outskirts of deep-soiled Carthage.'

'Carthage? I've never heard of it', Aeneas replied, taken somewhat aback by the forwardness of her greeting. 'Have you, Achates?'

Achates mumbled something indistinct, fearful as ever of committing a solecism.

'That's hardly surprising', the goddess continued. 'Carthage was founded only a few years ago. Its walls are still under construction. Even so, if I were a betting woman, I'd wager that it will dominate the Mediterranean one day.'

'What's the name of its king?' Aeneas asked, his curiosity piqued by this last comment.

'Queen, actually. A young widow by the name of Dido. She used to live in Tyre in Phoenicia. She's had a tough life, that's for sure. Her brother Pygmalion murdered her husband Sychaeus in order to acquire

VENUS AS HUNTRESS

Venus disguised as a huntress.

his wealth. Fortunately, Sychaeus had buried his treasure in the ground so rotten old Pygmalion didn't get an obol. He'd suspected that Pygmalion was up to no good, you see. Dido was devastated by his death. Sychaeus had been her childhood sweetheart. Dido knew her life was in danger, so she summoned her supporters, convinced them they would have a better life abroad, dug up the treasure, and hastily set sail. They settled in Carthage and the rest is history. Or at least it will be history one day.'

'A woman did all that?' Aeneas remarked admiringly, as much to himself as to Venus.

'She sure did', his mother replied.

'This Dido must be a very special person', Aeneas reflected. 'Women don't usually take matters into their own hands, even in the so-called modern world. We all know about the terracotta ceiling. I'd definitely like to meet her. I think we'd get on famously. I'm actually hoping to found a new city myself. Who knows, if things work out, perhaps we could join forces.' After a pause, he said hurriedly, 'But I'm getting ahead of myself. I apologise. I should have introduced myself. I'm a fugitive. I don't know how up-to-date you are with the latest news but the Trojan War ended some years ago. I was one of the mighty heroes who fought in it. I'm actually of semi-divine ancestry. My mother happens to be—'

But before he could say another word laughter-loving Venus had divested herself of her disguise and appeared before him as his queenly mother in all her radiant glory. She resembled a being from another dimension, which of course she was. A dazzling light emanated from her glistening flesh, which was draped in gauzy lingerie that flickered in the sunlight before his rapt gaze.

The goddess smiled serenely – an action which caused both of her cheeks to dimple seductively. Then she placed a delicately tapering forefinger on her son's lips, while stroking his cheek with the fingers of her other hand.

'You mother happens to be standing in front of you', she interrupted in a husky voice. 'Proceed on your way with my blessing. Dido will give you a warm reception. I and Jupiter, who hurls the thunderbolt, give you our word.'

Saying which, she vanished as though through an invisible doorway.

The sacker of cities was shell-shocked, so to speak. 'Why do you always do this to me, mother?' he protested to the vacant sky. 'Why can't we ever have a proper conversation? You always abandon me when I need you most.'

He turned to his faithful companion, who looked as if he was about to say something of a consoling nature when they suddenly found themselves enveloped in a thick mist. This was extremely convenient because it enabled the two men to make their way to Carthage without arousing any suspicion. Eventually they caught sight of a gilded cupola, glinting in the sunlight, signalling they were approaching their destination.

They entered the city through the turreted main gate, from which a banner floated. Still unseen, they proceeded along a thoroughfare till they arrived at a temple of vast dimensions, dedicated to the goddess Juno. A frieze depicting major events from the Trojan War ran around the outside walls. Aeneas had to fight back his tears at the depiction of atrocities that had been perpetrated against his countrymen, such as the killing of old King Priam at an altar.

'Troy will be remembered forever, Achates', Aeneas whispered, choking back his tears. 'That means something, I suppose, even if it's scant recompense for all the lives that were lost.'

But before Achates had a chance to reply, to their immense surprise and joy they observed many of their compatriots who they thought had been drowned. They were in the company of a beautiful young woman with flaxen curls tumbling down the length of her back. Her eyes were bright blue with long curling lashes. She had dimpled cheeks, a long, aristocratic neck, a generous bosom, and small delicate hands. On her head she wore a diadem, which signalled she was a queen.

An elderly Trojan called Ilioneus was addressing her:

'We're refugees from Troy. We're on our way to a land called Hesperia. All we ask for is the means to repair our ships. They were shattered on the rocks. Then we'll be on our way. I wish you could meet our leader, Aeneas, the well-known sacker of cities. He's a remarkable chap. We'd all have died long ago if it hadn't been for him. He rallied us in our hour of need. But I fear he was drowned in last night's storm.'

'That's too bad', Dido replied with genuine sorrow. 'I could have used a bit of help running this place. There's so much work to be done when you're founding a new settlement. I don't have anyone I can trust. Plus there's that Iarbas creep, the Numidian next door. He's always pestering me to marry him. I keep putting him off, but if I flatly reject him, he'll invade my territory.'

Just then, lo and behold, the mist enveloping Aeneas and Achates suddenly lifted. A very emotional reunion now took place between Aeneas and Ilioneus and the rest of the Trojans.

'Forgive me, your majesty', Aeneas said, after he had finished weeping with joy. 'I should have introduced myself. I'm Aeneas – the fellow this chap was talking about a moment ago.'

Because Venus had sprinkled a magic restorative over him, Aeneas was looking exceedingly godlike. Dido almost swooned at the sight of him.

'Well, well, what a coincidence', she remarked breathlessly, her bosom heaving, struggling to keep her composure. 'Welcome to Carthage, stranger. Why don't you and your fellows come to my palace and enjoy some Phoenician hospitality? I bet you could all do with a square meal.'

The Trojans shouted their approval, whereupon Dido, accompanied by a large retinue of courtiers, set off with all due pomp and ceremony. Aeneas, walking beside her, marvelled at what he saw. Construction was going on apace. Long lines of heavily laden slaves grunted in rhythm as they bustled about their work, clambering up ladders and trotting along wooden scaffolding with bricks and cement.

Eventually the royal party approached a set of steps leading to a platform on which stood a magnificent palace. As they drew near, the giant doors mysteriously creaked open, flung aside by invisible hands.

Dido escorted Aeneas into a magnificent dining room lit by a plethora of torches. Its walls were hung with tapestries depicting hunting scenes picked out in gold thread. Couches with purple coverings appeared out of nowhere, whereupon the queen invited her guests to recline. Scantily clad slaves laid out a sumptuous meal on small tables, one in front of each couch, and poured frothy wine into gold goblets.

After the Trojans had satisfied their hunger and thirst, Dido inquired of Aeneas how it was that he had come to Carthage.

'Well, long story short, after escaping from Troy with my father, my son and my wife, I tragically lost my wife. I joined up with all the others who had managed to escape from the ruins of Troy and wandered over the Aegean Sea for several days before arriving on the island of Crete. I tried to found a settlement but many of my companions fell victim to plague, so I had to call the expedition off. Then we sailed to the Strophades, which are inhabited by the foul Harpies who shoot poisonous arrows from their bottoms. Rather recklessly, I went scouting for rhubarb, for which the islands are famous, as you no doubt know. I had just come upon a very promising rhubarb patch beside a pond with ducks and bulrushes when the Harpies turned up in force and unleashed their disgusting weapons. I scarpered back to the ships. After that we sailed to the island inhabited by the Cyclopes, giants with a single eye in the centre of their foreheads. It turned out that Ulysses had been there a month earlier on his way home and blinded one of them. Then we sailed to Sicily, where, I'm sad to say, my dear father died of old age. After giving him a hero's burial, we set sail for Hesperia but were blown south to Libya. So here I am. I'm sure I've left some things out. My head's in a bit of a fuzz.'

Dido was mesmerised by his narrative. She had hung on every word. She would have hung on his lips if she could.

'I'm so sorry you lost both your wife and your father', she said at last. 'That must be so hard. But at least you have a son.'

'Ascanius, yes. He's a regular chip off the old block, as the saying goes. I left him with my men. But I still feel bad about my wife.'

'I'd love to meet your little boy', Dido said excitedly, clapping her hands. 'Please tell one of your men to bring him here.'

While they were awaiting his arrival, Venus, who had been observing their interaction with interest, abducted Ascanius and substituted Cupid. Even Aeneas couldn't tell the difference between the impish deity and his own flesh and blood.

'What a handsome boy!' she exclaimed when Ascanius' lookalike was presented to her. Instantly she clasped him to her breast. Cupid didn't

Harpies.

lose a moment. He pierced her bosom with one of his arrows, causing her heart to miss several beats.

Before she knew what had hit her, Dido was hopelessly in love. It didn't all go one way, however. Aeneas, likewise, was captivated by her charms, as well as by the tender way in which the queen doted on the fake Ascanius, and felt an equally powerful attraction.

Dido still had her feet on the ground, however. She was very much attached to her dead husband Sychaeus. She was aware, too, of the danger of succumbing to a rebound relationship. She decided to take her younger sister Anna into her confidence, without revealing the full depths of her emotions.

'I'm in a bit of a quandary, Anna', she casually informed her, while submitting to the expert ministrations of a dark-skinned slave girl who was giving her a much-needed pedicure. 'On the face of it, it seems as if this stranger could be Mr Right. He's handsome, brave, polite, god-fearing, pious – always a good quality in a man – charismatic, energetic, enterprising, has a good sense of humour, and, last but not least, he's unattached. You've seen us together. We hit it off pretty well, wouldn't you say? At the same time, I still have powerful feelings for

Cupid.

Sychaeus. I promised myself I'd never betray the memory of him. The thing is, however, I also have a responsibility towards my people. The Carthaginians would surely benefit from having a tested warrior like Aeneas to defend them against hostile attack.' Dido paused to let her words sink in. Then she asked, seemingly innocently, 'What would you do in my position?'

'I say go for it, Dido', replied Anna, who understood full well that her sister was seeking approval for initiating a relationship with Aeneas. 'You need someone to lighten your load. It makes sense on so many levels to get married again. Those wretched Numidians are just itching to get their dirty paws on your kingdom. You'd be doing us all a favour. Plus, you're lonely. You can't go on mourning Sychaeus indefinitely. You're still young. You have your whole life ahead of you.'

'OK, that's very helpful. I'll give what you say some thought', Dido replied, still putting up a show of resistance.

'You do that. But don't take too long making up your mind. A chap like Aeneas isn't going to stick around forever. He's on a mission. You can see it in his eyes. He needs to settle his people somewhere and it might as well be here as anywhere. Remember, too, if you want to start a family, your biological sundial is ticking.'

'True', Dido agreed, producing an involuntary smile. 'And we'd have the cutest baby ever.'

Anna had given Dido the permission she was seeking. She took the plunge that evening at dinner, while Aeneas was tucking into a plate of plovers' eggs smothered in honey – a speciality of the palace kitchen.

'Why don't we go hunting tomorrow?' she suggested, trying to sound as nonchalant as she could about it. 'It would be good for Ascanius to get some fresh air. He's been cooped up in the palace for days. A young lad like him needs to flex his muscles.'

Dido didn't want to make it look as if she was asking Aeneas out on a date. Women, not even queens, weren't permitted to take the initiative back in those days.

'Sounds like a plan', Aeneas replied enthusiastically, before popping the last plover's egg into his mouth.

When dawn broke the next day, however, the sky was overcast.

'There's a seventy-five per cent chance of rain', the seer Palamedes, a fellow with a gigantic goitre that hung from his neck in the form of a dewlap, announced prophetically.

Dido.

'I say we go ahead anyway', said Dido. 'We don't want to disappoint Ascanius. I know he's looking forward to getting on a horse. Besides, there are plenty of caves we can shelter in, if there's a downpour.'

After a hearty breakfast consisting of steak and salted fish topped with sows' udders, Dido and Aeneas returned to their separate quarters and hastily flung on their hunting gear. All the nobility of Carthage had turned out to give their queen a royal send-off.

Dido was mounted on a brightly caparisoned Arabian charger with a crimson saddle cloth, a silver bit in its mouth and silver studs on its harness. A plume was mounted on its forehead. She wore a purple tunic emblazoned with gold thread. A gold diadem studded with diamonds adorned her head, while pink highlights added drama to her curly blond hair. Thigh-length leather boots completed her gay apparel. Aeneas just couldn't take his eyes off her.

The pair hadn't been out for more than half an hour when the clouds began to amass and threaten. Suddenly the heavens opened and hailstones as big as your hand began pelting down, bouncing back up as they hit the ground.

Yet again, the storm wasn't unprompted. As soon as Juno had found out that her protégée and Aeneas were going hunting, she decided the best way to thwart Jupiter's plan was by arranging their marriage.

'Don't you think it would be nice if the Carthaginians and the Trojans formed one race?' she inquired of Venus.

'What a splendid idea!' Venus replied, professing enthusiasm.

Venus read Juno's mind perfectly. She had no intention of allowing her son to shack up with a semi-barbarous barbarian. He had bigger fish to fry. However, she decided to go along with the suggestion so that Aeneas would at least be safe in the short term.

'There's a cave over here', Dido exclaimed as the hailstones became even bigger and bounced even higher.

They galloped alongside each other, dismounted, and hastily entered the cave. A carpet of plushy sward fronted the entrance to the cave.

'We seem to have lost the others', Aeneas observed, shaking hailstones out of his hair. 'I hope Ascanius is ok.' Then turning around, he exclaimed, 'Gosh, Dido! You're sopping wet. Here, let me take your dress – I mean your mantle.'

For a few moments they gazed silently at each other. A cocktail of perfumes assaulted their nostrils, sending their senses swooning and inducing mild intoxication. Without either of them knowing who had taken the first step, first Dido's mantle and then her dress fell slowly to the ground. Before the queen knew what had hit her, so to speak, Aeneas was smothering her long neck with kisses, while grasping in both hands her callipygian buttocks. Then he pressed his lips to hers.

'I love you, I love you', he declared somewhat recklessly, as things would turn out.

Pinning her to the wall of the cave, he forced his tongue into her cherry red mouth and laid a sweaty palm on her creamy thigh. Incapable of resistance, Dido, her heart thudding, sank to the floor and yielded to her ardent lover.

Theatrical ululations and lightning flashes accompanied their love-making. Eventually Aeneas rolled off, having adopted the missionary position. Dido shook particles of dirt from her hair, and they dressed discreetly with their backs turned towards each other.

'Hey, don't forget your diadem', Aeneas said, picking the object up from the floor of the cave. It had got a bit bent in the course of their rapturous embrace, and he straightened it out before handing it to her.

Dido placed it back on her head. Then, looking down, she inquired bashfully, 'Did you mean what you said?'

'Did I mean what?' Aeneas inquired, tightening his bootstraps.

'Just now when you said you loved me? Is it true?'

'Of course, it's true, Dido. Do you think I would lie to you? I'm not called pious for nothing.'

When they emerged from the cave, a little the worse for wear, they were struck by the dazzling whiteness of the sky. The storm was over and a pitiless sun was beating down from a cloudless sky.

Now that the ice was broken, so to speak, Dido and Aeneas began to hang out with each other regularly. Though cautious not to display signs of affection towards each other in public, it wasn't long before their affair had become the subject of tittle-tattle. And from the Carthaginians it spread to the Numidians.

'Aren't you incensed about what is going on in Carthage, O son of Cronus?', Iarbas complained to Jupiter in high dudgeon. 'A beastly foreigner is having an affair with the woman I intended to marry. I'm outraged. Frankly I can't see any point in sacrificing to you, if you're going to allow this kind of thing to go on. It's a damned disgrace.'

Iarbas' words stung the son of Cronus into action. He immediately dispatched Mercury to Carthage. The wingèd messenger found Aeneas lounging in his perfumed bed at the ancient equivalent of three in the afternoon.

'What in the name of all the blessed gods do you think you're doing?' the messenger god demanded, as he flew through his bedroom window.

'Have you completely forgotten your destiny? Here you are, helping lay the foundations of an alien city with no thought to your future and the future of your people, all at the beck and call of a – a woman? It's time to draw stumps. If you don't care about your own reputation, give some thought to young Ascanius. He won't thank you for having a no-hoper as a father. You've a job to do. Or has that inconvenient truth escaped you? You want some advice? Get out of here before the father of gods and men f**ks you over good and proper!'

'OK, OK', Aeneas replied, jumping out of bed and slipping his feet into a pair of oriental slippers, to which pink pom-poms were attached. 'I'm onto it. But what in the name of Hercules do I tell Dido? She'll go ballistic.'

'Not my problem', Mercury replied, whereupon he sped off back through the window into the upper atmosphere, propelled aloft by his wingèd sandals.

Aeneas thought long and hard how to break the news to Dido. In the end he chose the coward's way out. He decided to sneak off without saying a word. He summoned Achates and told him to make preparations to sail the next day.

Dido immediately discovered what was going on, of course. How could she not? You can't keep anything from a woman in love, as Virgil observed. She burst into Aeneas' bedroom with reddened eyes just as he was about to head down to the shore to supervise his men.

'So you've decided to abandon me?' she screamed. 'How could you? After all I've done for you! Taking you in when you were homeless. Giving shelter to your men. Playing the mother to that kid of yours. You're a cad. You take advantage of me and now you're planning to abandon me and you don't have the decency to offer any explanation. You've made me a laughing stock, Aeneas. My people will despise me. What am I saying? They despise me already for showing a foreigner such favour. I've sacrificed my reputation and now you casually discard me. But it isn't just my reputation I've lost. Iarbas is bound to invade. Can you imagine what he'll do to me once you've gone? You've destroyed my life. Call yourself Aeneas the pious? You're a disgrace to your race.'

'Dido, I –' Aeneas began.

'And in the dead of winter you're planning to leave?' she demanded, adopting a more plaintive tone. 'Am I that loathsome to you? Couldn't you have delayed your departure at least until the spring? I thought

I meant something to you. How could I have been so wrong? If I'd got pregnant, at least I'd have had a child growing up in the palace to remember you by. Then I wouldn't have felt so desolate.'

Dido collapsed onto his bed in a flood of tears. Aeneas resisted the temptation to show any affection, mindful as he was of Jupiter's stern command. One thing can so easily lead to another in a situation like this, he reflected.

'Look here', he said at last. 'You've actually got your life worked out. Your city, Carthage, is establishing its high walls. You mustn't begrudge my Trojans their future. If I had my way, of course I'd stay here with you. You've been more than hospitable. But I never said I'd marry you. We have to be clear about that. The thing is, I'm not a free agent. I'm under orders from Jupiter, father of gods and men. Only this morning Mercury paid me a call. He told me in no uncertain terms that I had to leave immediately. I saw him with my own eyes in this room, just as clearly as I see you now. I have to head to Italy straightaway, albeit against my will.'

Dido sat upright on the bed. She shot a fierce glance at Aeneas.

'I don't know what you take me for', she snarled. 'You must have a very low opinion of my intelligence. Mercury came to you this morning, you say? In this room? That's the most pathetic excuse I've ever heard. You actually think the blessed gods care about our relationship? You're a coward. I hope you die an agonising death.'

And with that she stormed out of the room.

For the rest of the day, looking down from a tower in her palace, the queen observed the frenzied activity on the shore, as the Trojans loaded their ships with grain. In the end she couldn't resist making one more effort to detain her lover. She knew she was humiliating herself but she didn't care. So, she paid a call on her beloved sister Anna.

'Dearest Anna', she began. 'You've always had a good relationship with Aeneas. Go to him, I beg you, and plead with him to stay just a little longer. Tell him I'm not asking him to marry me – I've given that idea up – I just want a bit more time so that I can, well, learn how to grieve. I won't stand in his way after that, tell him. That's a promise.'

Anna kissed her sister and agreed to do whatever she could to detain him. She was fearful Dido might become unhinged. She ran down to the shore where Aeneas was inspecting the ships to ensure they were shipshape, so to speak.

'My sister's suicidal', she said, drawing Aeneas aside. 'I'm not exaggerating. I've never seen her like this before. I know you have to be on your way but I beg you to delay your departure for a few days. I don't know what will happen to her otherwise.'

'Sorry, Anna, I've received my marching orders', Aeneas replied gruffly. 'I should have left long ago. I've explained all this to your sister already. Now please, leave. There's nothing more to say. I've got a lot to attend to, as you can see.'

Anna headed back despondently to the palace.

'Well?' Dido asked eagerly.

Her sister shook her head sadly. 'He's resolved', she said quietly with downcast eyes.

She expected Dido to erupt in a flood of tears but to her surprise she remained silent. She was calm, even though she looked deathly pale.

'So be it', Dido observed. 'It's better that he should have revealed his true colours now rather than later. Good riddance to bad rubbish. I hope he rots in Hades. What I need to do now is to get him out of my system. I'm going to curse him good and proper. It's going to be the biggest, meanest, nastiest, most powerful curse of all time. I'll collect all the personal belongings that he left behind in his haste to get away from me and make a huge bonfire. It'll be a symbolic funeral pyre. Then I'll burn it all and I'll be rid of him forever.'

'Oh, Dido, I'm so relieved', Anna exclaimed, giving her sister a warm hug. 'I was so afraid. I thought you were going to hit the roof, but you're showing amazing fortitude and self-control. I'll go and give orders for a bonfire to be built in the courtyard.'

That night Aeneas slept on board his ship. He was planning to set sail as soon as Phoebus stepped into his chariot and cracked his whip the next morning. While it was still dark, however, Mercury appeared to him once again.

'How many times do I need to tell you to get out of here?' the god demanded exasperatedly. 'If you don't set sail immediately, the Carthaginians will burn your ships and take you and all your men prisoner. Dido's unpredictable – like all women. And then you'll be right royally screwed.'

Aeneas leapt out of his hammock. He gave orders to his men to raise the masts, hoist the sails and slash the moorings. By the time

31

rosy-fingered dawn showed her face, the Trojan ships were ploughing through the cresting waves.

Dido knew instantly the ships set sail. Observing the departing fleet with its brightly-coloured streamers fluttering in the wind, she let rip with the full force of her lungs:

'O sun, O Juno, O Hecate, O Erebus, O Chaos, hear my prayer! If it is destined for this abhorrent scumbag to reach dry land, may misery and suffering dog him all the days of his life, and may enmity exist for all time between his people and my people. And may an avenger one day arise to punish his descendants in generations to come!'

So saying, the queen ran to the courtyard of the palace and clambered on top of the bonfire on which were stacked all Aeneas' belongings. Grasping his sword, she slid it out of its scabbard and plunged it deep into her heart. A shower of blood jetted from the gurgling wound. She fell back onto the stacked logs beneath her, breathing stertorously.

It wasn't long before word of what had happened was spreading throughout the city. Anna dashed into the courtyard and climbed onto the pyre just as her sister was about to breathe her last.

'How could you do this? How could you deceive me like this?' Anna sobbed desperately, placing her sister's limp body in her lap and trying vainly to staunch the flow of blood.

Dido tried to raise herself up onto her elbow to acknowledge her sister but as she did so the blade, still stuck in the wound, made a grating sound against her breastbone. Wincing with pain, she fell back.

It's a law of nature that the immortal gods avoid the dying for fear of becoming contaminated by the pollution that their expiration causes. For that reason, gods are incapable of consoling mortals in their final moments. However, Dido's death agony was observed by Juno, who in pity dispatched swift-footed Iris to relieve her suffering, since Persephone, queen of the Underworld, is reluctant to receive those who die before their allotted time. Iris snipped off a tress of Dido's hair as an offering to the goddess and in an instant the life force departed from her.

Chapter 3

A Visit to the Land of the Dead

'Do you see those flames rising from what I think is the palace?' Aeneas asked Achates, pointing towards the shore, as his ship sailed away with an even keel parting the surge, lost from view in the shimmering haze, the clear blue water lapping against its bows. 'I wonder what that's all about. Any thoughts?'

Before Achates had a chance to reply, however, the helmsman Palinurus called out to Aeneas.

'A storm is brewing', he declared ominously. 'We're not going to be able to head directly to Hesperia. We'll have to sail to Sicily instead.'

'Sicily?' Aeneas repeated. 'Seems like it's déjà vu all over again.'

'I'm afraid so, boss', Palinurus replied.

The voyage took them till late afternoon the next day.

'There's a sandy beach over there', Palinurus said when they eventually reached the western tip of the island. 'I suggest we head for it.'

'Unless I'm very much mistaken that's the mound under which we buried my father' ashes', Aeneas replied, squinting through the rain. 'Come to think of it, it's the anniversary of his death tomorrow. It's pretty obvious that the blessed gods must have planned all this. They want us to pay him our respects. I vote we celebrate games in his honour – rowing, running, javelin throwing, archery and boxing. With any luck, it'll become an annual tradition.'

'Sounds like a plan', Palinurus agreed, steering the ship towards the beach.

On reaching dry land, the Trojans dragged all their ships onto the shore. Things didn't quite go as planned, however. Just when the Trojan youths were enacting a mock cavalry battle to conclude the games, Juno of the golden throne, still bent on causing havoc, again dispatched Iris, disguised this time as an old crone, to stir things up.

'I hate men', Iris exclaimed, shaking a gnarled fist and stamping her foot. 'They think only of themselves. Here they are, having their fun and games, while we have to scrub the decks, mend the sails, caulk the rotting timbers, scrape away the mould, not to mention do all the cooking and raise the kids. We've been sailing around the Mediterranean for seven whole years and we still haven't arrived in Hesperia? I say we settle here.'

The Trojan women eagerly agreed. They'd been feeling pretty disconsolate anyway at having been ignored in all the decision-making.

'There's only one way women can make men see reason', Iris went on, 'and that's by digging their metaphorical heels in.'

So saying, she picked up a burning log from a fire beside which the women had been warming themselves and hurled it with great force in the direction of the nearest ship. Instantly its timbers caught fire. All the women cheered and began following her example. Before long the fire was spreading from ship to ship.

As soon as they saw flames mounting into the sky from the direction of the shore, the Trojans interrupted their games and ran down to the shore. Each grabbed an amphora and began dousing the fires. The entire fleet would have been burnt to cinders, had not Jupiter, who sees all things, or at least most things some of the time, observed what was happening.

'What the –!' he exclaimed. 'This is Juno's work. That crazy woman is always trying to thwart me. I wish I'd never married her.'

At this, the father of gods and men leapt up from his throne, hastily gathered a bunch of rain clouds, and unleased a storm of almost unparalleled violence in the direction of Sicily.

Once the fires had been extinguished, Aeneas picked his way among the debris to examine the damage. Many ships were beyond repair but some were still seaworthy. Not for the first time he found himself wondering when all this misery would end. Perhaps the women were right. Why not settle in Sicily after all?

That night, however, his father appeared to him in a dream.

'Leave the bulk of your men here and take the best of them to Hesperia', Anchises advised. 'Ditch all the women. They'll only be a hindrance to you. You can always find women. Italy is your destination, not Sicily. Sicily is for sissies. Ha, ha, ha. First, however, you'll need to visit the Land of the Dead. You'll find the entrance at a place called Cumae, about halfway up the west coast. The local Sibyl will act as your guide. I'll meet you inside Pluto's realm. There are things I need

34

to tell you about the destiny of our race. Nice games by the way. Much appreciated.'

Greatly relieved to know that his father was still there for him, as the saying goes, the next day Aeneas took a refreshing matutinal shower under a waterfall in order to clear his head. Then he held a meeting.

'Listen up. I want only men who have a taste for adventure to accompany me to Hesperia. There are still many trials ahead. The rest of you are free to remain here in Sicily with the women.'

Having gathered together his volunteers, Aeneas ordered them to repair the ships and fit them with new sails and oars. Their work completed, they set sail for Cumae in the bay of Naples.

When Aeneas climbed up on deck around dawn on the second day of their voyage, however, Palinurus was nowhere to be seen and the ship was yawing perilously. He grabbed hold of the tiller just in time to avoid some rocks. Feathery sleep had enveloped the helmsman during the night. It happens.

Assisted by the Earthshaker, Aeneas directed his flotilla to Cumae without further mishap. On reaching dry land, the Trojans hauled their ships onto the beach. Then they thanked their lucky stars – and the gods – that they had finally arrived in Hesperia.

'OK, men, you stay here and take it easy', Aeneas ordered. 'I need to find the entrance to Hades. It must be somewhere around here.'

There was quite a bit of grumbling from the men, many of whom were seized by green fear at the mention of Hades, while others questioned his sanity, but Aeneas brushed their objections aside and set off.

Having inquired of a passerby as to the whereabouts of the local Sibyl, he was directed to a nearby cave. At the entrance he observed an elderly woman with matted hair and an angry-looking mole on her freckled nose, who was sitting cross-legged on a large stone, some two feet in diameter. She was foaming at the mouth, as is per normal in the case of Sibyls.

'Am I right in thinking you might be the local Sibyl?' Aeneas inquired.

'Indeed you are', the elderly woman replied in a plangent tone, wiping a gob of foam onto her grubby sleeve. 'And who might you be?'

'I'm pious Aeneas', Aeneas declared.

Hearing this, the Sibyl let out an ear-piercing cry and began shaking uncontrollably. Her eyes rolled upwards into her head so that only the whites were visible.

'Most unfortunate of mortals', she cried. 'Do you think you have reached safety just because you have survived the terrors of the deep? I see the River Tiber foaming with blood. Terrible, bone-crunching wars lie ahead for you. You will supplicate strangers for aid. Your descendants will be condemned to fighting endless wars. Evil will assail you on all sides. This is the price your descendants must pay for the peace they will bestow on the peoples they conquer.'

'Good to know', Aeneas replied, somewhat taken aback. 'I'm not entirely surprised. Nothing comes easily in this life. But I didn't come here for a prophecy. I'm here to visit my deceased father Anchises. He requested my presence. Could you show me the entrance to the Land of the Dead? I understand that three-bodied Hecate gave you the keys to their realm, so unless I'm very much mistaken it lies in your power to grant me access.'

'O, most ill-fated of mortals', the Sibyl replied sonorously. 'It's easy enough to enter Hades – you won't have any trouble on that leg of your journey – but not so easy to leave it. However, if you're bent on this course, heed my advice. First, you're going to need a golden bough. That's to give to Proserpina. She won't allow you to enter her realm otherwise. You'll find one in that forest of cypress trees over there', she said, pointing over her shoulder with an arthritic forefinger. 'Keep going straight and before long you'll reach foul-smelling Avernus, the birdless lake. "Avernus" derives from the Greek word *aornus*. Birds avoid the lake like the plague.'

'Will you act as my cicerone?' Aeneas asked.

The Sibyl stared at him blankly.

'I mean as my guide.'

She shook her blue jowls. 'I've given you all the directions you need.'

Aeneas was about to leave but the Sibyl suddenly grabbed hold of his wrist with her choppy fingers.

'Not so fast. Not so fast', she animadverted. 'First you have to sacrifice a black-fleeced lamb to Night and a barren heifer to Proserpina. You also have to sacrifice as many bulls as you can lay your hands on to the denizens of the dead.'

'That might be a trifle difficult', Aeneas replied, disengaging his arm from her claw. 'I've just got here, you see. In Hesperia I mean. Where in Hades' name do I get bulls from? Never mind a black-fleeced lamb and a barren heifer. I'll just have to chance it without the sacrifice.'

'Suit yourself', the Sibyl said with a nonchalant shrug. 'But you'll definitely need this.'

She handed him a grimy leather pouch.

'What's this for?' Aeneas asked, holding the soiled object at arm's length between thumb and forefinger.

'It contains three honey cakes laced with a sedative. You give them to the monstrous three-headed canine Cerberus. Otherwise he'll bite your head off – literally. Oh, and by the way, one of your men is lying unburied on the shore – a fellow by the name of Misenus.'

'Misenus? You mean Hector's brother-in-law?' Aeneas asked aghast. 'He was my favourite trumpeter. Boy, he could rouse the dead with a peerless blast of his instrument – metaphorically speaking. How did he die? He seemed in good health when I left my men a short while ago.'

'He took it upon himself to challenge the gods who live forever to a contest in trumpet-blowing. Arrogant sod! You'll need to give him his due rite of burial before he will be able to enter the Underworld.'

'Thanks for your help, Sibyl', Aeneas replied, 'I'm most appreciative.' Then he bowed gravely and departed.

Incidentally, I very much suspect that it was this particular Cumaean Sibyl whom Apollo fell in love with when she was a young girl. In return for agreeing to sleep with him, the god offered to give her anything she wanted. Pointing to a heap of sand, she asked to live as many years as it contained grains of sand. Then she promptly reneged on her promise. The god gave her a second chance, pointing out that she should have asked for perpetual youth instead of perpetual age, but still the girl refused him. Ageing all the while, she shrivelled and shrunk until eventually the priests of Apollo popped her into a glass bottle, and there she remains to this day. When Roman children come to look at her, they ask, 'Sibyl, what do you want?' to which she invariably replies, 'I want to die.'

When he got back to the ships, his men were standing in a circle around the corpse of Misenus.

'OK, I heard what happened. Start building a pyre sharpish.'

Their task completed, his men placed Misenus' body on top of the pyre and set fire to the faggots. Aeneas was musing absentmindedly upon the brevity of human existence as the flames devoured the corpse, when suddenly he became aware of a pair of doves hovering above him.

'Doves are sacred to my mother Venus', he exclaimed excitedly. 'She must have sent them to guide me to Hades. OK, keep stoking the pyre, men. Achates, I'm leaving you in charge.'

Aeneas headed in the direction where the doves, flitting constantly above his head, were leading him. He finally arrived at the aforementioned cypress wood. It was so dark that he could scarcely see his hand in front of his face but the constant chatter of the birds guided his steps. Eventually he perceived a tree that was sprouting branches of gold. He tore one of its branches off, whereupon the doves flew off. Shortly afterwards he found himself standing on the shore of what he concluded to be foul-smelling Avernus.

Ahead of him was a porch made of somber-looking black stones, which, he further surmised, marked the forbidding entrance to the Land of the Dead.

As soon as he stepped over the threshold, he was assailed by an assortment of hideous personifications, foremost among whom were Disease, Old Age, Famine and War. There, too, were the Furies, who wreak vengeance on those who have murdered their close relatives. Various monsters, such as hundred-handed Briareus, three-bodied Geryon, and the Chimaera who spits out jets of flame, tried to block his path, but he gallantly fought his way through all these impediments with thrusts of his trusty sword.

Eventually he found himself on the shores of the Styx, the river which encircles Hades. An elderly man, bald except for strands of hair sprouting from the back of his neck, with a stained and yellowing beard, dressed in a filthy brown smock that barely covered his bony knees, was standing in a waterlogged boat. He was clutching a tall pole that rose several feet out of the sludgy water. Aeneas instantly recognised him to be Charon, the ferryman of the weightless dead. A vast throng of departed souls was queuing up to get aboard his frail barque. Aeneas elbowed his way to the head of the queue. Being bodiless wraiths lacking substantiality, they couldn't put up much resistance, so they sought to deter him by making shrill bat-like noises that pierced his eardrums.

'Not so fast', said Charon, glaring menacingly at the queue-jumper. 'Where in Pluto's name do you think you're going? You go to the back and wait your turn like the rest. If you don't behave yourself, I'll make you wait a hundred years.'

'Is that so?' Aeneas replied menacingly, standing his ground. 'Then take a look at this.'

Whereupon, from under his cloak, he produced the golden bough, which flashed in the inspissated gloom.

Charon's jaw dropped. With a single sweep of his arm, he casually shoved the insubstantial dead who were seated on thwarts in his barque into the water and Aeneas clambered awkwardly aboard. For a few seconds it seemed as if the boat was about to sink from his weight. At this all the dead gibbered, fearing that they would be left stranded on the shore outside Hades for all eternity.

Aeneas sat down, careful to distribute his weight evenly. Using his pole, the ferryman eased off from the shore. For about twenty minutes, he powered his craft through the slimy ooze at what seemed to Aeneas to be the speed of light. Eventually they arrived on the far side of the River Styx, where Charon deposited his earthly passenger.

'That'll cost you an obol', the old man said, extending his greasy hand.

'Next time', Aeneas replied, brushing his hand aside and clambering up onto the muddy strand.

Out of nowhere a slavering three-headed mastiff appeared and began snapping ferociously at his ankles.

'You must be Cerberus', he said, crouching to pat each of the creature's three heads in turn. 'I've got a little present for you. Here, try this.'

Whereupon he opened the little leather pouch which the Sibyl had given him and proffered the honey cakes to the mastiff. All three mouths of all three heads began gobbling greedily. Before long the animal was snoring contentedly.

Numerous shades appeared before him, classified according to the manner of their death. The first category he met were infants, dead before their lives had begun. Next were suicides. Next came those who took their own lives because of a broken heart. Suddenly he caught sight of Dido.

'Ye gods!' Aeneas cried out, genuinely upset. 'What are you doing down here, Dido? I hope you didn't take your life because of me. Like I told you before I left, I wasn't a free agent. I want you to know I still have feelings for you. I always will.'

Dido gave him a scornful glance, turned her back on him, and evaporated into the surrounding mist without uttering a syllable. As she did so, Aeneas caught sight of what he took to be the ghost of her husband Sychaeus. He was touched to see that they were holding hands.

He shook his head despairingly. 'Why did it have to be me whom the Fates singled out as the instrument of their will? Why couldn't I have

39

Cerberus eagerly awaits new arrivals in Hades.

married Dido and settled down in Carthage? Instead, here I am, trudging through this sunless region, surrounded by gibbering ghosts and hideous monsters, still searching for a home. It's simply not fair.'

Just then he caught sight of a former comrade-in-arms called Deiphobus, a son of King Priam. He was horribly disfigured. Both his hands had been chopped off, his ears had been ripped off, and his nose was missing.

Aeneas was dumbstruck. 'What happened?' he asked softly.

'It's all due to that accursed Helen', Deiphobus replied bitterly. 'I married her after Paris was killed, as you know. It was she who betrayed us to the Greeks. The night we brought the wooden horse into the city, she led the Trojan women in a dance of celebration. A dance of death more like. The blazing torch she held aloft gave the signal to the Greeks that it was safe to enter the city. Then she led Menelaus and Ulysses into my bedroom and this is what they did to me.'

40

Aeneas wanted to question Deiphobus further, but at that moment he caught sight of his father's shade dressed in a long white gown. He ran towards him eagerly, arms outstretched. Just as he was on the point of embracing him, however, he passed straight through him.

'What the –!' Aeneas exclaimed, coming to a shuddering halt and turning around.

'The dead can't have any physical contact with the living', Anchises explained. 'We lack substance. Don't you know that?'

'Of course, I do', Aeneas replied. 'In my eagerness at seeing you I forgot you were vacuous. I got carried away, so to speak. Literally.'

'Anyway, it's good to see you, boyo', Anchises said brusquely, eager not to display too much emotion. 'There's not a lot going on down here. I thought you'd never come. I'll show you the sights. Then I'll give you some tips about what lies ahead for you and your Trojan buddies.'

Father and son chatted inconsequentially for a few minutes before they came to a fork in the road.

'This is where Hades divides', Anchises explained. 'If you take the left turn, you'll end up in a bottomless pit surrounded by a river of fire – the Phlegethon. It's called Tartarus. But we're going to take the right turn. This one leads to Elysium.'

'Did you just say Tartarus? Isn't that where all the damned abide?' Aeneas inquired. 'I've heard of it. Who's that foul creature with puss oozing from her eyeballs – she has gigantic dugs, so I assume she's a female – seated at what I take to be the threshold of the bottomless pit?'

'That's the avenger Tisiphone. Tisiphone works for Rhadamanthys, the judge of the dead. Once Rhadamanthys has determined you belong

Tartarus.

41

in Tartarus, Tisiphone grabs you with her blood-stained claws and boots you down into that giant sinkhole. There's no exit, so you'll be there for all eternity. The Titans are down there – the primeval offspring of Earth who tried to overthrow Jupiter, the god whose voice is borne afar. So are all those other monsters of depravity, like Tityos and Ixion.'

'Who's Tityos?'

'Tityos tried to rape Leto, the mother of Apollo and Diana.'

'And Ixion? What was his crime?'

'He tried to rape Juno.'

'So, sex offenders end up here?'

'Not only sex offenders. There are also parricides, adulterers, traitors, oath-breakers, et cetera, et cetera – all the worst kind of criminals. You name it, they're down there. Their punishments are dreadful. Sisyphus, for instance, has to push a huge rock uphill. Just as he gets it to the top, the rock rolls back down and he has to go through the whole damn process again. And again. Ixion is nailed to a constantly revolving wheel with his arms and legs spread-eagled.'

'I think I've seen enough to last me an eternal lifetime', Aeneas quipped.

'Ha, ha, very funny', Anchises said. 'If I had sides, they'd be splitting with laughter. Anyway, it's time we moved on. You can only stay here so long as Aurora is driving her rosy chariot through the sky, and I still have something important to show you. By the way, you see that palace over there? That's where Proserpina lives. That golden bough you're clutching – just leave it on the threshold. Then she won't be offended because one of the living has entered her kingdom.'

'That's quite a palace', Aeneas remarked, depositing the bough on the topmost step, while staring up at its towers. 'Who built it?'

'The Cyclopes.'

'You mean those fellows with a single eye in the centre of their foreheads? I thought they were pretty stupid.'

'Well, they aren't. They're highly skilled craftsmen. There isn't much about breaking off massive rocks and smashing them into pieces that they don't know.'

Suddenly the darkness began to lift and Aeneas found himself in a sunlit meadow. A gentle breeze was blowing and there was a fragrance in the air. Some people were singing and dancing, others were exercising.

'Where are we now?' Aeneas inquired.

'This is where the Blessed Ones live', Anchises replied. 'It's called Elysium.'

'What do you have to do to become blessed?'

'You have to have lived in the Age of Heroes.'

'So, if you were born in the Age of Iron as we were, you can't be blessed? That doesn't seem fair.'

'Oh, I almost forgot, poets live here as well.'

'Why poets?'

'No idea. I suppose it has something to do with the belief that poets are inspired by the Muses.'

'And who are those ghosts who are swarming around that river over there?'

'They're waiting to drink from the waters of Lethe. *Lethe* is the Greek for forgetfulness. Once they've drunk and forgotten their past lives and paid for their crimes by spending one thousand years in purgatory, they can return to earth and be reborn.'

'You're kidding. You mean some people want to live twice? I can't imagine anything more pointless. Been there, done that. Isn't that what people say?'

'OK, this is what I wanted to show you', Anchises went on, ignoring this remark. 'You see that crowd of hazily articulated figures standing solemnly in line in the far distance?'

'Yes. Who are they? They look burdened with gravitas.'

'They're your biological and cultural descendants, son. They're waiting their turn to be born. The fellow who is standing at the head of the queue is Romulus. Much further down you can see a bald-headed man. That's Julius Caesar. He'll be descended from Venus, like you. It's in your gift to summon all these people to life by fulfilling your destiny. If you roll your dice right, one day your progeny will found a city called Rome and many centuries later Rome will rule the world. It'll become the greatest city on the face of the earth. You should feel extremely proud to be selected for such an undertaking. It's not going to be an easy task and the Romans won't get much thanks for it. But they'll make it safe for people to sleep in their beds at night. That's no mean feat, given the general state of the world these days. Romans aren't going to be world-class sculptors in bronze and marble or astronomers or lawyers. They'll leave all that to the Greeks. Instead they will teach nations to practise peace. That will be their special skill set, so to speak. They'll do it by sparing the conquered and subduing the arrogant.'

Aeneas stood silently, looking at the long line of generations yet to be born. He knew that his father was eager to bolster his courage and give justification for the trials he faced ahead. Try as he might, however, the future meant nothing to him. It was like looking down the wrong end of a telescope, not that he knew what a telescope was. All he could do was shake his head in bafflement and wonder.

'Well, I never', he said at last.

'My sentiments precisely', said Anchises. 'Shall we go?'

Father and son made their way slowly back to the entrance. Anchises continued to talk enthusiastically about the mission his son would accomplish. Aeneas nodded from time to time but said nothing. He couldn't get Dido out of his mind. Eventually they reached the Gates of Sleep. One gate is made of horn, the other of ivory. If you pass through the gate of horn, you have true dreams. If you pass through the gate of ivory, your dreams are false.

'This is where we must part', Anchises said. 'Farewell, son.'

'Farewell, dad', Aeneas replied. 'It was quite a trip, in both senses of the word. I feel my consciousness has been exponentially expanded.'

So saying, he passed through the gate of ivory into the upper air, into the realm of the insubstantially substantial.

Was his visit to the Underworld merely a figment of his imagination? Or is the world of harsh and unforgiving sunlight to which he returned itself the world of the imagination? Do we merely observe the imaginary reflection of an imaginary world?

The poet Lucretius memorably described Cerberus, Charon, Pluto and Proserpina and all those other mythological beings that put fear into the hearts of men and women as 'pure mumbo jumbo'.

'Death', he remarked philosophically in his great epic poem *On the Nature of Things*, 'is merely the dismembering of the particular collection of atoms that constitutes temporarily our physical being. Once you're a goner, you're a goner. *Kaput*, lights out, *finis*. Even the dust to which we belong is mutable. And yet religion induces people to do terrible things in the name of their gods.'

Or words to that effect.

Or in the words of a pithy Roman epitaph: 'I wasn't, then I was, now I'm not, and I don't give a damn.'

Chapter 4

The Trojans Arrive in Hesperia

As soon as he returned to the sunlight realm, Aeneas ordered his companions to set sail without further ado. A favouring wind drove them north and before they knew it they had arrived in the region known today as Tuscany. They beached their ships, disembarked, furled the sails, and stowed the masts as per normal. They would never have to use them ever again.

'I don't know about you, but I'm starving', said a man with a scar that passed from his brow down the entire length of his right cheek.

'Me too', enthusiastically replied a man whose nose had been eaten away. 'I could eat a horse. But what do we do for tables?'

'Why don't we lay the food out on loaves of bread?' a one-eyed man whose left arm ended in a stump suggested, emitting a somber eructation in anticipation.

It was clear that Aeneas' men had, as the saying goes, been in the wars.

Just then a group of wild hogs passed by. Quick as a flash, Aeneas whipped an arrow from his quiver and hit one smartly on the snout. The creature fell to the ground. Its little feet wriggled and its tail twitched, but only for an instant. His men speared it, roasted it and began devouring the flesh heartily. There wasn't a lot to go around, however, and before long they were devouring the bread as well.

'Look, we're eating our tables!' squealed Ascanius, who had become something of a smart alec of late.

Aeneas' jaw dropped. 'In the name of the Heavenly Twins!' he exclaimed. 'This must be Latium. We've arrived, we've finally arrived at our destination – the end of all our wanderings! We're here! We've made it! Long ago I heard a prophecy from Priam's son Helenus that we would put down roots at the place where we began gnawing the tables we were eating off. I thought it meant we would be starving. It all goes to show how mind-bendingly obscure prophecies can be.'

A whoop of joy arose from the men and they began dancing on the sand ecstatically.

'We need to find out who's the ruler of this land', Aeneas said. 'Ilioneus, I'm putting you in charge of the embassy. Take a hundred men with you. Make sure you all wear garlands made of olive branches as a sign you come in peace. We don't want to give the wrong impression. That tall building in the distance looks like it could be a palace. I suggest you make inquiries there. From the looks of things the owner must be pretty powerful. You can present him with Priam's robes. They're stored in a chest in the hold of my ship. In the meantime, I'll get the lads building an encampment. I suspect we'll be here some time.'

Ilioneus ordered one of the men to fetch the chest and soon afterwards he and the other ambassadors set off in the direction of the palace.

They seem to have been expected. No sooner had they mounted the steps than the doors swung open before them and the guard on duty ushered them down a long corridor into the throne room.

Seated on the throne was a diminutive white-haired man in his fifties. His slippered feet dangled several inches off the ground. He had a kindly smile on his face, which put Ilioneus immediately at ease.

'I know who you are. You're Trojans, right?' the diminutive man said. 'What are you doing here? You're a long way from home.'

'I and my fellow Trojans are refugees', Ilioneus replied, going down on one knee, as did all the other ambassadors. 'It's true that news travels

THE PROPHETIC SOW AND HER LITTER.

The prophetic sow and her litter.

slowly in the modern world but I feel sure you must have heard that Troy was destroyed seven years ago. We – that is to say, our leader Aeneas – was wondering if you might grant us a plot of land where we could settle. We won't cause any trouble. Apparently, there's some decree or oracle or whatnot that says we're destined to settle in these parts. So, we're rather hoping that you might look favourably on our request. If you do, we'll become your allies in any future war. We're valiant and tested fighters.'

Ilioneus ordered the chest to be placed on the floor and opened the lid.

'Aeneas bade me offer you these robes with his compliments. They once belonged to King Priam. May I inquire whom it is I have the honour of addressing?'

'My name is Latinus', the little man replied, leaning forward to examine the contents of the chest. 'I'm the eponymous king of Latium, the region in which you now find yourself. Latium was once ruled by Saturn in the so-called Golden Age. It's where agriculture was first practised on the face of the earth.'

'Your majesty', Ilioneus said, inclining his head with a broad sweep of his arm.

Latinus snapped his fingers and a slave stepped forward smartly. He closed the lid, picked up the chest, and departed.

'Tell Aeneas to come and plead his case in person', the little king said. 'I'll be pleased to meet him. I have a feeling things will work out between our two peoples. It so happens that I have a daughter called Lavinia. My father, who happens to be Faunus, god of forests and fields, prophesied to me recently that she would marry a foreigner. Who knows, maybe this prophecy is about to come true. The only problem is that Turnus, the prince of the Rutulians, wants to marry her. Turnus is very jealous. If I give away Lavinia to a foreigner, he'll probably start World War One. But we'll meet that bridge when we come to it. In the meantime, tell your leader that the Trojans are welcome to reside in Latium, so long as they don't cause any trouble. Oh, and thank him for the robes. I'll have them shortened.'

Ilioneus rose to his feet, exited the palace at the head of the embassy, and hurried back to the ships. On arrival, he breathlessly told Aeneas all that had happened.

'Well, it sounds like we've kicked off to a good start here', Aeneas remarked, scratching his chin thoughtfully.

He couldn't have been more wrong.

Latinus had been hoping to keep the report of his conversation with Ilioneus secret for the time being. Unfortunately, it had not gone unnoticed by Juno, who even at this late date was still hell bent on opposing the Trojans in every way she could. To cause divisiveness among the Latins, she now dispatched a particularly objectionable minion of hers called Allecto to spread news of Aeneas' arrival to Amata ('Beloved'), Latinus' wife.

That night Aeneas was visited in his sleep by Father Tiber, who informed him that he should look out for a huge white sow which had just farrowed thirty piglets lying beside a secluded river under a holm oak tree as further proof of the fact that he had finally reached the end of his travels.

'There are storms gathering ahead', the river god added. 'I suggest you go and request help from King Evander, a Greek who settled in Hesperia. He lives a few miles inland.'

'Can anyone see a huge white sow lying under a holm oak tree close to that river over there that has just farrowed thirty piglets?' Aeneas demanded early next morning.

'Over here!' the man whose left arm ended in a stump exclaimed, holding up a squealing piglet by its curly tail in his one remaining hand.

'Well done, that man!' Aeneas exclaimed. 'Our next job is to find a fellow called Evander. He lives upstream somewhere. I suggest we make a woodskin canoe. We don't want to attract too much attention. I'll need a few volunteers.'

Evander's palace turned out to be situated on top of the Palatine Hill. In this way Aeneas and his companions visited the future site of Rome without realising it.

'Take my son Pallas and his pals', Evander replied, when Aeneas asked if he could lend him some military assistance. 'He's a valiant fighter. Mind you take good care of him.'

Whenever anyone says that before sending a young man off to war, you know it's a bad sign. And so it proved.

In the interim Allecto had entered Amata's boudoir, coiled herself around her ankles like a snake, and was literally dripping poison into her ear. Amata had a soft spot for Turnus and when she learned that her husband was casting him aside in favour of some random stranger, she threw a fit. Instantly she flounced into the throne room, her dander seriously aroused.

'How could you possibly contemplate such a thing!' she screamed. 'You want our daughter to marry a common refugee? Just wait till Turnus hears about this. He'll not take this sitting down. On the contrary, he'll make war on you, you mark my words. You'll destroy Latium, if you give our daughter away. Is that the legacy you want to leave behind?'

'I just want peace', Latinus said dolefully, absentmindedly tugging at his earlobe, his little legs swaying nervously back and forth. 'I hate war.'

'You don't deserve to be a king', Amata observed with a sneer. 'If you've got any sense, you'll tell the Trojans to get back in their ships and leave this land immediately.'

So saying, she turned on her heel and again flounced, though this time out of the throne room, slamming the door loudly behind her.

Shortly afterwards Latinus retired to his private quarters. The argument with his wife had brought on a fearsome migraine. He didn't have the stomach for a domestic brawl, so he informed his chief advisors that he was declaring war against the Trojans.

Turnus, having found out that Latinus had initially promised Lavinia to Aeneas, was determined to teach the foreigner a lesson. Accordingly, he summoned all the greatest warriors in Italy and, allied with the Latins, prepared for all-out war.

When the Trojans learned that they would have to fight for their survival, they were cast into something close to despair. Just when they thought their travails were over, they were facing a life-or-death struggle.

Being vastly outnumbered, Aeneas went off in search of more allies to join his cause. As soon as he had departed, Juno dispatched swift-footed Iris to inform Turnus that the coast was clear. Turnus called the Rutulians to arms and launched an attack on the Trojan camp.

The Trojans were completely unprepared. Even so, they defended themselves valorously. The tide of battle went back and forth.

After much blood had been spilled, the two heroes agreed to decide matters by single combat. Turnus was no match for Aeneas, however. When he smote Aeneas' shield, the blade of his sword shattered.

Juno looked down on the action, tears in her eyes. She'd given it her best shot and there was nothing more she could do.

'It's time to admit defeat', observed the father of gods and men, patting his wife on the back affectionately.

'OK, but on one condition', Juno replied, trying her best to put a brave face on things.

'Name it.'

'That the Trojans agree to be called Latins.'

'Agreed', Jupiter replied with a nod of his head, which action caused a mighty thunder clap to burst forth.

Aeneas aimed his spear and hurled it at Turnus with all his force. The missile whizzed through the air like a tornado and struck the edge of his shield. It pierced his breastplate low down and ripped through his thigh. Turnus fell on one knee, clutching his leg in excruciating pain. A howl of anguish rang out from the Latins. Aeneas ran forward and stood towering above his foe, glaring down at him through the eye-slits in his helmet.

'Have pity on me', Turnus pleaded, stretching out his hand. 'Or at least have pity on my parents. If you won't spare me, promise me you will return my dead body to them.'

Aeneas was suddenly reminded of his father. He was about to yield to Turnus' request when he saw that he was sporting – 'sporting' is exactly the word to use in this context because that's the word that occurred to Aeneas – a fancy leather belt that had belonged to Evander's son Pallas, whom Turnus had recently slain.

All instinct to show compassion deserted him and with all the strength at his command Aeneas plunged his sword deep into Turnus' breast. His spirit, sighing reluctantly, joined the numberless shades below.

Aeneas and Lavinia were married soon after. Nothing is known of their life together. Was theirs merely a marriage of convenience? The only thing we know is that Aeneas named the settlement that he founded in Latium 'Lavinium' in her honour.

Universal peace didn't break out even now, however, and the inhabitants of Lavinium – united as a single people – were fated to fight many wars. Some years later Aeneas met his death while fighting – again – against the Rutulians. His body was never recovered and the story circulated that he had been taken up onto Olympus. Whether that was true or false, a cult was established in his honour.

Ascanius was still a minor when his father died, so Lavinia reigned until he came of age. It's greatly to her credit that she successfully warded off all the military threats that the city faced from neighbouring peoples. In due course she abdicated in his favour.

The population of Lavinium increased rapidly under Ascanius' rule so that he found it necessary to establish a settlement in the Alban Hills called Alba Longa, meaning 'The Long White City'.

The death of Turnus (after Pietro da Cortona).

All that we know about Alba Longa is a mysterious story relating to the Heavenly Twins, Castor and Pollux. It is said that Ascanius built a temple in Alba Longa to accommodate a pair of statues of the gods which had been formerly housed in Lavinium. One morning, however, a priest opened the doors of their new temple only to find that the statues were missing. They had somehow made it back to their old pedestals in Lavinium. The statues were brought back to Alba Longa but to no avail. Exactly the same thing happened again. Eventually it was decided to let them reside in Lavinium, since this was what the Heavenly Twins wanted.

After a long line of kings of no consequence, a quarrel broke out between Numitor and Amulius, the sons of an Alban king called Proca, destined to alter the course of history.

Chapter 5

Romulus Founds Rome

When King Proca died, Numitor, his elder son, should have inherited the throne. Instead, his younger son Amulius staged a palace coup. Amulius had Numitor's two sons murdered and forced his daughter, a rather high-strung and self-willed girl called Rhea Silvia, to become a Vestal Virgin. If a Vestal Virgin breaks her vow of chastity, she's condemned to death. In other words, Amulius had condemned his niece to a life of perpetual virginity.

Some months after Rhea Silvia had taken her oath, it became obvious to all that she was pregnant. Amulius was furious. He summoned his niece to appear before him.

'Vestal Virgins must remain virgins!' he thundered, banging his fist on the arm of his throne. His nostrils flared and there were hectic patches on his cheeks. 'That's the whole point of being a Vestal Virgin. It's not asking much, is it? You're a disgrace to your sacred order. Well, you asked for it. You know the rules. You leave me with no choice. Guards, take her away and bury her alive!'

'It wasn't my fault', Rhea Silvia replied flatly. 'I was raped.'

'That makes no difference. A victim of rape is always guilty in the eyes of the law on the grounds that she should have – or rather could have – resisted her attacker. You know that as well as I do. It's physically impossible to violate any woman against her will. By breaking your sacred oath, you've imperilled the safety of Alba Longa. That's a capital offence.'

I should point out that the notion that it was impossible to violate a woman against her will was standard Roman belief for hundreds of years.

'But what if the rapist happens to be a god?' Rhea Silvia demanded coolly.

'What do you mean?' asked Amulius, taken aback.

'My rapist was Mars.'

'Don't try and pull that one on me', Amulius sneered. 'Do you take me for an idiot?'

A Vestal Virgin.

'It's the truth. I'll take a mighty oath to that effect if you want. Mars came to me during the second watch of the night and had his way with me. I could hardly resist a god.'

'You're lying', Amulius said cautiously.

'OK, if you don't believe me, go ahead. Bury me alive. But if my offspring happens to be fathered by Mars, I certainly wouldn't want to be in your sandals.'

Amulius bit his lip. He didn't believe Rhea Silvia but he couldn't entirely rule out the possibility. Stranger things have been known to happen.

'OK, throw her into prison', he told his guards begrudgingly. 'I hope you rot there.'

Four months later Rhea Silvia gave birth to twins, later to be named Romulus and Remus. When Amulius found out, he decided to expose them. This way the elements would be to blame for their death. What if Mars actually *was* the father? It was best not to take any risks.

Accordingly, he summoned two of his most trusted henchmen, bow-legged ne'er-do-wells with deeply sunken eyes and villainously low foreheads.

'Toss these brats into the River Tiber where its current runs strongest', he commanded, handing the man a wicker basket, in which the twins were innocently sleeping.

It so happened, however, that Fate chose to intervene, as it does so often in mortal affairs. On the present occasion, it took the form of a torrential downpour that began as soon as the henchmen stepped out of the palace and began plodding bow-leggedly towards the river. Within minutes the Tiber had burst its banks and was flooding the land on both sides. The henchmen were thus unable to detect the course of the river. After excogitating for some while, they both waded into the flood and left the basket as close to what they guessed to be its course as they could.

Some hours later Fate intervened in our story again – this time in the form of a she-wolf that had recently lost all her cubs.

The basket containing the twins had been carried downstream by the flood waters and once the waters had retreated, it fetched up beside a wild fig tree. The infants, having awoken, now began crying lustily. Their cries were heard by the she-wolf, which graciously decided to put her swollen dugs to good use. The animal gently picked the twins up in her slathering maw and bore them to a nearby cave, later named the Lupercal, at the foot of the Palatine, one of Rome's seven hills. She lay down and offered them her teats. The two boys were famished and began sucking greedily.

Not long afterwards a herdsman happened to pass by the cave – yet another intervention by Fate – or, conceivably in this case, merely a stroke of luck.

'Well I never', the herdsman, whose name was Faustulus, exclaimed, impressed by the tender way in which the she-wolf was licking the infants with her pink tongue.

The she-wolf suckles Romulus and Remus.

Though the animal seemed to be doing a good job, Faustulus deemed it his duty to take control of the situation. He picked up a large stone and threw it at the she-wolf. It struck her rib cage. She gave a yelp of pain and slunk off, abandoning her charge.

That's the last time I'll take pity on a human, the she-wolf reflected bitterly.

Faustulus gathered up the twins, one in each arm, and carried them home to his wife, Larentia. They were poor folk and dwelt in what might fittingly be called a hovel. A small, moth-eaten blanket was all the twins possessed for covering, so there was nothing to indicate their royal background. It so happened (yet again) that Larentia had recently given birth to a stillborn child, so she was more than happy to offer her teats to the boys, just like the she-wolf had offered hers. Once again, the twins were starving so they consumed her milk equally greedily, oblivious to the fact that it was human as opposed to lupine.

It was thus Faustulus and Larentia who named the boys Romulus and Remus.

Understandably some Romans have found the story of the she-wolf highly implausible. So they came up with an alternative version. They claimed that there was a prostitute nicknamed Lupa, who lived in the area where the twins were found. *Lupa* is the Latin for 'she-wolf'. It also happens to be the Latin equivalent for the colloquialism 'hooker'. According to this version of the story, therefore, Romulus and Remus were rescued not by a she-wolf but by a prostitute.

Whatever the truth of the matter, the boys grew to lusty manhood, never doubting for one moment that they were the sons of Faustulus and Larentia. Around the age of sixteen, they joined a gang of robbers, as boys from a lowly background commonly did in those days. They were good robbers, however. They didn't rob the poor. They only robbed people who had previously robbed other people. Or at least that's what the Romans who fashioned this story claimed, not wanting to suggest that their ancestors were common criminals.

'We've got to teach these hooligans a lesson they won't forget', said one hardened robber to another, after he had just been robbed by the gang presided over by Romulus and Remus.

'What have you in mind?' his fellow-robber inquired.

'A festival known as the Lupercalia takes place on the Palatine Hill in three days' time. Romulus and Remus are bound to attend. I suggest we kidnap them and turn them over to Amulius for punishment. With any luck he'll have them executed and we'll be able to get on with our robbing as before.'

'OK, let's do it', his companion agreed enthusiastically.

The Lupercalia festival, which was held in honour of a shadowy figure called Lupercal, began with the sacrifice of several goats and a dog. After the thigh pieces of the victims had been offered to the gods, the priest distributed the rest of the meat among the celebrants. This was followed by a curious ritual. The skins of the victims were cut into leather strips and handed to all the youths who were present. The women of child-bearing years formed a circle and the youths ran past, flicking them with their leather strips. This action, it was believed, greatly increased their fecundity.

As soon as Romulus and Remus ran past, the robbers leapt out from the crowd and hauled them off, brandishing long knives to deter anyone who tried to stop them. Romulus managed to escape, but the robbers successfully kidnapped Remus by tying his arms behind his back.

Romulus and Remus.

The next day, with their captive in tow, they sought an audience with Amulius.

'We accuse this man of terrorising the locals, your majesty', the chief robber said.

'What crimes has he committed?' Amulius demanded, smacking his lips appreciatively. He liked nothing better than to have a justifiable reason to indulge his taste for inflicting cruel and unusual punishment.

The robber thought for a moment. 'Well, terrorising, like I said. Remus, here, and his brother have been thieving. Romulus evaded us. He needs to be apprehended ASAP.'

'What have they been thieving?' the king inquired.

'Horned cattle. Lots of horned cattle. Horses as well. Oh, and a flock or two of sheep. Short-bristled pigs, too, I believe.'

'I haven't heard of any short-bristled pigs being stolen recently', Amulius remarked. 'Or cattle. Or horses for that matter. Horned cattle are always going missing though.'

'The pigs were the property of your brother Numitor', the robber stated.

'Very well. Hand this fellow over to Numitor for punishment. I'll come and watch to see it's being meted out correctly.'

The robber gave Remus a kick and led him away.

In the meantime, Romulus had rushed home to tell his parents what had happened.

'Mum, dad, Remus has been kidnapped!' he shouted breathlessly, bursting through the door of their rat-infested hovel with its low mossy roof.

Faustulus and Larentia were both horrified. Larentia dropped the dough she had been kneading on the rush matting. After Romulus had finished his account, the two exchanged knowing glances.

'There's something we've been meaning to tell you for a long time, Romulus my boy', Faustulus remarked somewhat awkwardly. 'I suppose this is as good a time as any.'

'What is it?' Romulus asked.

'Larentia and I aren't actually your mum and dad.'

'Not my mum and dad? What do you mean? Who are my mum and dad then?'

'We don't actually know', replied Faustulus. 'I found you, you see. Someone placed you and your brother in a basket and cast the basket into the Tiber. It's a long story. I'll tell you it another time. Anyway, your mother and I have been noticing lately that you and Remus aren't like the other boys around here. You have – how can I phrase it? – a kingly bearing.'

'A kingly bearing? What do you mean by that?'

'Our suspicion – it's only a suspicion, mind you – is that you're the sons of Rhea Silvia, that unfortunate Vestal Virgin who claimed she was raped by Mars.'

Romulus furrowed his brow and pondered for a few moments.

'You mean Remus and I could be the grandsons of Numitor?' he inquired at last.

'Yes, and quite possibly the sons of Mars.'

'Mars', Romulus repeated, as he took the revelation in. 'Wow.'

It so happened that Numitor had reached the same conclusion at the exact same time. As soon as Remus was brought before him, he, too, was struck by his kingly bearing.

'How old are you, laddie?' he inquired of him shrewdly.

'I've just turned sixteen.'

'And you have a twin brother, I understand?'

'Yes, a brother called Romulus [Little Rome].'

'And your father is a herdsman, you say?'

'That's right.'

'I need to have a word with him.'

Numitor sent a messenger to Faustulus, requesting to see him immediately. Once the truth came to light and all was revealed, an emotional scene took place. The twins informed their grandfather that they were going to restore him to the throne. Numitor was overjoyed. He notified his supporters, who placed themselves under the youths' command.

The youths then launched an attack on the palace. Most of Amulius' supporters deserted him and he died in the assault. Once the citizens of Alba Longa had acknowledged him as their rightful king, Numitor made an announcement.

'I have some important information. I've decided to abdicate. I appoint these lads here, my grandsons Romulus and Remus, as joint rulers in my place. I also order the immediate release from prison of my daughter, Rhea Silvia.'

Joint rule has never been a very successful system of government, however, and so it proved on this occasion.

Not long after, Romulus happened to remark to his brother, 'Have you noticed how crowded the streets have become lately?'

'Funny you should mention that', replied Remus. 'I have indeed noticed it. Why do you suppose that is?'

'Alba Longa is experiencing a demographic explosion.'

'What's a demographic explosion?' asked Remus.

'It means the population is increasing dramatically due to an accelerating birthrate', Romulus explained.

'Got it', Remus replied. 'What's the solution?'

'We have to do the same thing that our forefather Ascanius did when Lavinium experienced a demographic explosion. We have to found a new city.'

'Got it', Remus said again. 'Can I be the king?'

'No, you jolly well can't. You'll stay here and rule Alba Longa. You've always wanted to rule it by yourself. Well, now's your chance. I've already identified the site for the new city. And besides, I'm older than you.'

'By a hair's breadth', Remus objected. 'Besides, you and I both know that Alba Longa is no longer the place it once was. It's becoming a shithole. I think we should toss for it.'

'Toss for it?' Romulus repeated derisively. 'That's a stupid idea. The only reasonable solution is to let the gods decide. We'll ask them to send us a sign. You can watch from the Aventine Hill and I'll watch from the Palatine.'

Remus agreed, and before dawn the next day each of the brothers, accompanied by their supporters, took up his position, each on his designated hill.

They didn't have long to wait. Just as the sun was rising, six vultures appeared to Remus flying over the Aventine Hill, so named from the Latin word *avispicium*, which means 'looking for signs from birds'. All his supporters started cheering wildly. They were on the point of declaring him king, when a similar cheer rang out from Romulus' supporters on the Palatine Hill. They'd just seen twelve vultures overhead.

Both sides descended to level ground, each declaring themselves to be the winner. Before long an angry altercation had broken out.

'I told you we should have tossed for it', Remus commented petulantly.

'Well, twelve beats six, so you lose', Romulus snarled belligerently. 'Sod off back to Alba Longa.'

Reluctantly Remus and his supporters backed down. Romulus didn't waste any time. The very next day he ordered his men to begin building a wall around the area he had marked out as his new settlement.

'I'm calling the city Rome', Romulus announced.

When Remus heard that the building project was underway, he became curious to inspect it. The truth was that he was dying of jealousy.

'You call this a wall?' he jeered, contemptuously kicking the bottom course with his boot. 'You think that'll protect you against the enemy? Dream on. This is just a pathetic excuse for a city.'

'The wall is just begun, dope head', Romulus responded angrily. 'Keep away, little brother. You're not welcome here.'

'Not welcome?' Remus said with a smirk. 'Is that so? What are you going to do about it, I wonder? Guess what, I'll lay siege to your city.'

So saying, he jumped over the wall and made a rude gesture.

'Look, I've broken through your defences!' he exclaimed, laughing.

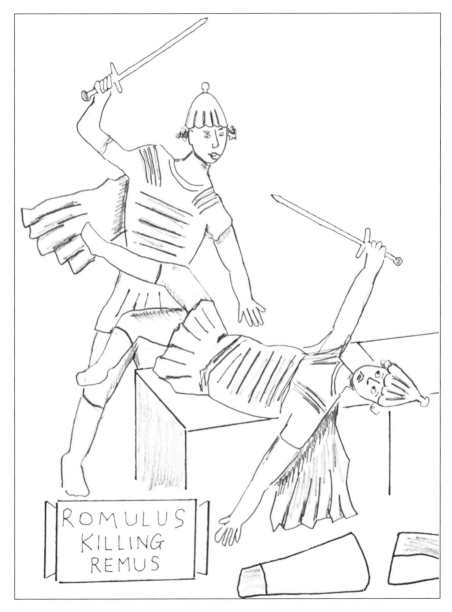

The death of Remus (after Augustyn Mirys).

Romulus was furious. Without a moment's delay, he drew his sword from its sheath and plunged it into his brother's stomach, taking the wind completely out of his sails, as one might say.

Remus fell on his face and expired. A pool of blood spread in a wide circle beneath his body.

'So perish anyone else who dares to jump over these walls', Romulus declared pithily, glancing around menacingly at the shocked bystanders.

No one took up the challenge.

Romulus had chosen well. Rome is situated at the first easy crossing point on the River Tiber, some fifteen miles from the coast as the crow flies. A small island, called Tiber Island, facilitates the crossing. Its distance from the sea makes it safe from pirates. It lies on the Via Salaria or Salt Route, so there's a lot of salt available, a vital commodity. Its seven hills, of which the largest is the Capitoline, provide ideal defence under attack and refuge whenever the Tiber floods its banks – a frequent occurrence.

So this was how Romulus became the first king of Rome – by an act of fratricide. Not many people in the history of the world have been prepared to acknowledge that their founder happened to be fratricidal, but the Romans did not shield themselves from this unpalatable, not to say unpalatinable, truth.

Chapter 6

The Sabine Women Intervene

Romulus' main task was to increase the size of Rome's population so that it would eventually dwarf that of Alba Longa. To achieve this end, he did everything he could to attract outsiders. He didn't care what type of person settled in his city. He set up an asylum inside its walls where anyone who wished could apply for residency, irrespective of their background. Soon the word got about that if you were a fugitive from the law or an exile or a refugee or a homeless person or merely down on your luck, Rome was the place for you. The city grew from strength to strength. Before long, it was fast outstripping Alba Longa in size.

There was a problem, however. The majority of the asylum seekers who flocked to the city were men and this was causing a huge gender imbalance. To address this problem, Romulus sent envoys to all the nearby towns, asking whether they had any females who were surplus to requirements, as the envoys tactfully put it.

Wherever the envoys went, however, they were met with scorn and contempt.

'Rome is where all the lowlifes live', the neighbouring peoples replied. 'It's full of cut-throats and psychopaths and sociopaths. We don't want anything to do with the place. We wouldn't hand over our daughters to you if you were the last men alive. You're scum. Get out of here, before we set our dogs on you.'

When the envoys dejectedly returned and described how they'd been treated, Romulus was, as the saying goes, incandescent with rage.

'I'll get even with those sons of bastards!' he exclaimed, stamping his foot. 'They think we Romans are scum? I'll teach those braggarts a lesson.'

For days Romulus stormed around the *regia* or palace, effing and blasting, uncertain how to respond.

A word about the *regia*. This was a wedge-shaped building located in the centre of the Roman Forum. The front part contained a shrine to Mars, god of war, because the king, who dwelt there, was also the commander-in-chief. At the back of the building was a temple to Ops, the goddess who personified Wealth. The *regia* housed the state archive, called the *annales*, which recorded all the monstrous events that occurred from year to year. This included reports of pigs being born with human heads, never a good sign. In later times the building also stored the official texts of the numerous prayers and vows that were recited from time to time, as well as a copy of the religious calendar, known as the *fasti*. The *fasti* were extremely complicated because the Romans had to placate so many gods.

Even back in Romulus' day the *regia* exuded a terrific sense of what the Romans called *religio loci,* which roughly translates as a 'sense of religion'. This is hardly surprising, since the building was literally bursting at the seams with all kinds of minor deities who resided in it.

One day, after tearing his hair out in search of a solution, Romulus had a brainwave. He summoned the Chief Pontiff, a wizened old man called Postumus with thin spindly legs, a rotund belly, hollow cheeks and a single incisor that projected horizontally from his lower jaw.

'Your reverence', Romulus said, slapping the priest affably on the back. 'I've decided to establish a new festival.'

'A new festival? In whose honour, O mighty one?'

'A festival in honour of Consus, the god who protects the grain that is stored in our granaries. It's to be called the Consualia. I want you to make preparations for it straightaway.'

'Is there any particular reason for the haste?' Postumus inquired, scratching a suppurating boil on the tip of his nose. 'Normally it takes a while for a new festival to be set up. We'll have to consult the Cumaean Sibyl for a start. Every religious innovation has to be ratified, as you know.'

'I don't give a toss about the Cumaean Sibyl. I had a dream last night. I dreamed that if we don't establish a festival in honour of Consus immediately, he'll come down on us like a ton of bricks. Not to put too fine a point on things, we'll be bollocksed.'

'Bollocksed?' Postumus repeated, cupping a shrivelled ear with his bloated right hand to make sure he had heard properly. 'He surely didn't use that word, did he?'

'He jolly well did', Romulus affirmed. 'The god was very open with me. You'd better not waste any time. Consus wants the festival to be celebrated as soon as possible and he wants it to be on a grand scale.

He said he's fed up being ignored by us when all he ever does is give, give, give. Giving stored grain, that is. Or rather protecting stored grain. From mould and mildew, as you know. You're to push the boat out. No holding back. Got it? By the way I want you to send out invitations to all the neighbouring towns inviting them to come and witness the festival. It'll be an opportunity to impress the locals. It's about time they took us seriously. We'll host them so that they can stay over for the duration of the festival. It's your job to see to that as well. Well, get going, man. There's no time to lose. By the way, make sure you invite the Sabines. Tell them to bring their wives and children. They'll be particularly welcome.'

Postumus shuffled off. Once out in the sunlight, he felt a sharp stabbing pain in his chest. Over the next few weeks he worked day and night, making preparations and sending out invitations. Sadly he dropped down dead two days before the Consualia was due to be celebrated. This might have been considered a bad omen, but Romulus took the news in his stride.

'Consus has taken Postumus to his bosom', he announced breezily to the other priests. 'It's a sign that the god is pleased with our honouring of him. We must make sure the festival in his honour is an especially magnificent affair.'

What Romulus didn't tell the priesthood was that the festival was merely a ploy to solve the chronic shortage of women.

Visitors, including many Sabines, began pouring into the city from miles around. Greeters standing at the gates first welcomed them and then conducted them to their lodgings. They also took them on tours so they could inspect the fortifications and the layout of the new city.

On the day of the festival, the celebrants gathered outside the city to witness a chariot race between four teams of horses. At a pre-arranged signal, and when the race was at its height, the Roman youth, who had distributed themselves among the visitors, grabbed hold of all the Sabine women of child-bearing age and dragged them off screaming to their separate houses. For the most part it was a matter of first-come-first-served, though Rome's senators had earmarked the most beautiful women in advance.

The Sabine men were outraged but found themselves powerless to intervene, since they had come unarmed to witness religious festivities. This made the action of the Romans all the more offensive in their eyes. Cursing, they took to their heels and fled.

Although this incident is always referred to as the 'rape' of the Sabines, the Romans saw it more as an abduction. After all, the women, or so they claimed, weren't actually raped. Once they had been separated from their families, so the story goes, they quickly adjusted to their new living conditions. The problem is that the Latin word for 'rape', *rapio*, also means 'seize or abduct'. Anyway, the historian Livy claims that what the Romans really wanted was to marry the Sabine women and start families with them.

Even though the incident leaves a bad taste in the mouth, it's noteworthy that later Romans were eager to believe that their ancestors conducted themselves civilly. Accordingly, they claimed that the youths immediately declared undying love for their wives-to-be and that in a remarkably short space of time their feelings were reciprocated. What initiated this change in heart was, they suggested, the charm offensive which Romulus began undertaking the next day, visiting one by one every household that had acquired a Sabine woman.

'Now look here, young lady', Romulus would begin soothingly, patting the young woman in question on the back. 'I know this has come as a bit of a shock and you're probably feeling somewhat disorientated, not to say discombobulated, but I'm here to assure you that you're not here to satisfy the lust of this young man here.' Then, turning to the young man, he would say, 'Right, Marcus?' – or Sextus or Lucius or Postumus or Decimus or whoever it might be. 'No-one intends you any harm, least of all dear old Marcus here. But Rome, in case you don't know, happens to have a dearth of women. The city needs to increase its population. We're hoping you'll play your part in that. If you want to blame anyone for your present condition, blame your parents. They were too cocky to permit intermarriage with their neighbours. You're certainly not here *just* to be a breeder. You're here to fulfil the role of wife and helpmeet. In turn for your services, you'll be granted all the rights and privileges that go with that status. Henceforth you'll share in the fortunes of Rome. And in time to come, you and our lads will be united by the precious bond of parenthood. In other words, it's a win-win situation for all concerned.'

Legend has it that Romulus' pleas smoothed their ruffled feathers and the Sabine women accepted their new identity with a good grace. There were some grumblings of discontent from those who were betrothed already, but before long the majority had taken to their new life with relish. Rome had its advantages even back then. It was already a thriving city with a number of well-appointed villas, shops selling luxury items, and – it's signature attribute, one might say – hot baths. The Sabines by contrast lived in smelly hovels, subsisted on a diet of weeds and root vegetables, and rarely if ever saw a bar of soap.

I should perhaps add that Rome had by now begun to succumb to viciousness, corruption and frivolity, like all major cities the world over throughout history, but that is strictly beside the point and not a part of our story.

Just when the women were getting comfortably settled, however, their parents and brothers started stirring things up. A group of them presented themselves outside the palace of the Sabine king, Titus Tatius, angrily demanding an audience. They were accompanied by an assortment of ambassadors from neighbouring settlements.

'Surely you aren't going to let the Romans get away with this affront to our dignity, are you?' they demanded, after the king had granted them an audience.

'Of course I'm not!' Titus retorted sharply. 'What do you take me for? I happen to have bribed a Roman girl called Tarpeia, the daughter of a certain Spurius Tarpeius, the commander of the garrison on the Capitoline Hill. Tarpeia knows a secret entrance that will enable our troops to gain access to the fortress. The plan is to make an assault on the citadel tonight. I didn't want word to leak out. That's why I didn't tell you.'

The ambassadors congratulated the king on his forethought and departed.

That evening Tarpeia admitted the Sabines and their allies into the fortress that crowned the Capitoline Hill. The Roman guards were taken completely by surprise.

History does not record what Tarpeia's motive was in betraying her own people. Irrespective, the girl came to a justifiably sticky end. When the Sabines asked her what she would like for delivering the fortress into their hands, she replied, 'The things you've got on your arms.' What she meant was their jeweled bracelets. Instead, the Sabines clubbed her to death with their shields.

In later times, the rock by which the Sabines had ascended became the place where traitors and condemned criminals stood before being tossed to an agonising and lingering death. Named the Tarpeian Rock, it bore the eternal memory of the girl's falsehood.

Early next morning the Romans tried unsuccessfully to re-take the citadel, while bitter fighting broke out between the Palatine and Capitoline hills.

As the fighting became more intense, a group of Sabine women thrust their way between the two armies, driving them apart.

The most eloquent of these women now addressed the Sabine soldiers as follows:

'Our newborn babies are either your grandchildren or your brothers or your sisters or your nephews or your nieces. Please bear that in mind as you raise your swords.' Then turning to the Romans she cried, 'We have sacrificed all our familial ties for the sake of your city. But the men you see before you are our fathers and our brothers. Would you strike them down?' Finally to all she said in a measured tone, 'Forget all the grievances of the past. Sabines and Romans have the chance to forge a single destiny and live peaceably alongside one another. If you persist in killing each other here today, your blood will cry out from the ground for all time.'

The intervention of the Sabine women (after Picasso and Jacques-Louis David).

Silence fell on both sides. Then, quietly at first but with gathering volume and at last deafeningly, both armies began cheering the women. Romans and Sabines alike sheathed their swords and embraced. The commanders on both sides stepped forward and a formal cessation of hostilities was declared.

The next day Romulus and Titus Tatius met to thrash out the details of what they hoped would be an enduring peace. They agreed to merge the two peoples under a single constitution with two kings. As a gesture of goodwill to their neighbours, the Romans even agreed to call themselves 'Quirites', which derived from a Sabine town called Cures. Though 'Quirites' eventually fell out of daily use, it was employed in formal contexts to describe the citizens of Rome. They also named the districts into which Romulus divided the city for administrative purposes after Sabine women. Incidentally, Tatius died at the hands of a violent mob not long afterwards. Such was life back then.

This was the last of Romulus' acts of which we have record. Soon afterwards he died as well. The cause of his death is disputed. One explanation is that he ascended into the sky during a thunderstorm. Another, which his detractors disseminated, is that a bunch of senators tore him into very small pieces.

Just when it seemed as if the two sides contesting the nature of his demise were about to come to blows, a respected Alban farmer named Julius Proculus came forward and addressed the populace in the Campus Martius, the Field of Mars, the place where assemblies are held.

'Quirites', Proculus exclaimed, 'Romulus, the founding father of our beloved city, hearing of the bickering that has resulted from his departure, descended from his seat in the sky at dawn this morning and appeared before me. He instructed me to inform you that Rome is destined to become the most powerful city in the world. So long as we fight our enemies and avoid the curse of civil war, no harm can ever come to us. I was about to ask him for further details about Rome's future, but before I could get a word in, he had ascended into the sky again. I may be a country bumpkin, but I know a god when I see one.'

The populace took comfort from Proculus' words in the confident belief that a man of his integrity would never lie.

Chapter 7

The Horatii Save Rome

After the death of Romulus, the Romans chose Numa Pompilius as their second king. Roman kingship wasn't hereditary. On the contrary, it was an elected office. What is surprising about the choice is that Numa was a Sabine. Inevitably there were objections from those who thought his appointment would give the Sabines undue influence but no other candidate of suitable qualifications came forward and Numa was duly elected *nem. con.*

Numa was very smart. He was so smart in fact that he outwitted Jupiter. One day, a strong wind began shaking the branches of the trees on the Aventine Hill. Moments later there was a terrific thud as of a weighty object hitting the earth and the father of gods and men appeared. Initially Numa was petrified – who wouldn't be? His heart began beating faster, his hair stood on end, his blood ran cold, and he began shaking like a proverbial leaf. However, he valiantly stood his ground.

'Son of Cronus', he began, 'to what do I owe this unparalleled honour?'

'I've come to demand a sacrifice.'

'Your wish is my command', Numa replied, bowing low. 'I shall be more than happy to oblige, but might I be so bold as to ask for something in return?'

'You may be so bold', Jupiter replied. 'Whether I will grant your request is another matter altogether.'

'OK, here goes. I'd like some advice about how to expiate your lightning strikes so that the ground they strike isn't forever cursed. The thing is, whenever you release one of your thunderbolts at some perjurer who has sworn falsely in your name, we regard the spot that you strike to be unusable, and since you've been striking quite a lot of perjurers lately, it would be extremely helpful if we could come to some agreement whereby the land can be made available again.'

'Very well, I will allow this, but in turn you must do something for me. You will have to cut off a head.'

'No problem', replied Numa, thinking quickly. 'I'll dig up an onion and cut it off from its roots.'

'Either you don't get what I meant or you're being deliberately obtuse', Jupiter observed testily. 'What I meant was I want you to cut off a human head.'

'OK, I'll cut off the hair of a human head', Numa replied without a moment's hesitation.

'I want a life, you obdurate fellow!' Jupiter snapped.

'By all means, O mighty one. I'll give you the life of a fish.'

Jupiter's eyes blazed. He raised a clenched fist and was just about to bomb Rome back into the Stone Age when he suddenly broke into a smile.

'OK, I admit I'm beaten', he said. 'In future, when you want to expiate my lightning strikes, remember to sacrifice an onion, some human hair, and a fish.'

The following day Numa summoned the populace and prayed to Jupiter to provide proof that the agreement he had made with him was binding for all time. In response, an earsplitting thunderclap boomed forth. Moments later a shield with a convex curve on either side landed at Numa's feet with a clatter.

'This means we shall always be victorious in war', Numa announced triumphantly. Then raising his arms skyward he intoned, 'Thanks, almighty Jupiter.'

In case anyone tried to steal the original, Numa ordered Rome's most gifted metalworkers to fashion eleven identical shields, similar to the one that had fallen from the sky. For added protection, he also appointed a college of self-styled Leaping Priests to protect the shields. Every year, before the campaigning season begins in March, the priests perform a curious dance involving leaping. They also chant an obscure hymn – so obscure in fact that no one actually understands what it means. Indeed it is doubtful whether the priests themselves understand its meaning.

In other ways Numa made it his task to establish Rome on a secure religious footing. The worship of the gods had existed in the time of Romulus, but there was a lot of confusion about what form observance should take in order to propitiate the gods. For the purpose of acquiring knowledge of religious lore, Numa, who was by now an old man, had nightly assignations with a nymph called Egeria, who resided in a grotto beside a stream on the outskirts of the city.

NUMA and EGERIA

Numa Pompilius and the nymph Egeria reorganise the Roman calendar.

Under her guidance, Numa organised a festal calendar listing all Rome's sacrifices and other religious observances, which he divided into twelve lunar months. This, of course, was hardly an ideal solution, since twelve lunar months fall eleven days short of the solar year, which meant that every few years an extra month had to be added or intercalated to bring the calendar back in line. In later times a lot of calendrical conniving took place, enabling magistrates to insert an extra month in order to prolong their time in office. Not until Julius Caesar came along was the problem fixed once and for all.

It was Numa who established the practice of appointing Vestal Virgins, though, as we've seen, they seem already to have existed in Alba Longa. He also erected a temple in honour of two-headed Janus, the god of gates and doors, after whom the month of January, Latin *Ianuarius*, is named. Numa decreed that the doors of Janus' temple should be closed in time of peace and open in time of war. Closed throughout his reign, they remained perpetually open for seven hundred years until the first Emperor Augustus established the *pax Romana*.

It was inevitable that these nightly assignations soon became the subject of malign gossip. Tittle-tattlers began saying that the superannuated king was using religion as an excuse to have a clandestine affair with a young girl. There was even a report that Numa had secretly married Egeria. Whether there was a shred of truth in these rumours is unknown.

Two-headed Janus.

Numa was succeeded by Rome's third king, Tullus Hostilius. Like Romulus and Remus, Tullus had been brought up by shepherds. One of his most notable acts was the building of Rome's first Senate house, the eponymous *Curia Hostilia*. I forgot to mention that the Senate had been established under Romulus as an advisory body and that it was the Senate which elected the king.

Tullus hadn't been long on the throne when a quarrel broke out between Rome and Alba Longa. In response, the Alban king, Mettius Fufetius, invited Tullus to a parley.

'Look here, old boy', Mettius said jovially. 'This is crazy. We're both Trojans by ancestry. Our common patriarch is Aeneas. That's one reason to bury the hatchet. But there's another, even more pressing reason right now. I don't know whether you've noticed it, but the Etruscans, the people who live north of the River Tiber, have been rattling their swords lately. They'd like nothing better than for us to engage in hostilities and weaken each other. Then they'd swoop down and finish us both off. I suggest we appoint two champions to represent us. That way there will be minimal blood spilt between us.'

Tullus tugged at his beard thoughtfully. 'Hmm, that's not a bad idea. It's true that the Etruscans have been looking very belligerent recently.'

'I don't suppose you have any triplets by any chance?' Mettius inquired.

'Triplets? Funny you should ask', Tullus replied. 'We do as a matter of fact. One set. The Horatii brothers. Fine strapping young men. Why do you ask?'

'We have a set of triplets too. My lot are called the Curiatii. Equally fine strapping young men. Let's put them to fight each other.'

The two kings shook hands on the deal and a date was fixed for the contest. Tullus, being very warlike, was a bit disappointed that he wouldn't get a chance to test his mettle, but he saw the wisdom of Mettius' suggestion.

The only problem was that the two sets of triplets were already related by marriage. In fact, a sister of the Horatii, a girl named Camilla, was engaged to one of the Curiatii.

The day of the contest rolled round. The Horatii swore on their father's life that they would lay down their lives in the service of their country, as did the Curiatii.

Just as the anticrepuscular rays of Helios were bursting forth from behind the Alban Hills, the six champions took their stand midway

THE OATH OF THE HORATII

The oath of the Horatii (after Jacques-Louis David).

between Rome and Alba Longa. The rival armies were lined up behind them. Tullus and Mettius performed a sacrifice and swore to abide by the result of the competition.

Soon blood began to flow on both sides. First one Curiatii was wounded, then a second, and finally a third. Their wounds weren't lethal, however, and they were able to continue to fight with vigour and determination. First one and then another Horatii hit the dust, close-girdled in iron sleep, never to rise again.

Publius, the last surviving Horatii, was, however, uninjured. He retreated to recover his breath. All three Curiatii pursued him, now severely weakened from the loss of blood. Suddenly he turned and charged at his leading adversary. He plunged his sword into his heart, whereupon darkness clouded the man's eyes and he crashed to the ground. A loud cheer rang out from the Roman army. Moments later he felled the second Curiatii, and soon after the third.

HELIOS
THE SUN GOD

Helios.

The Romans were exultant. Mettius admitted defeat and acknowledged the subjection of Alba Longa to Rome.

A domestic tragedy marred the Roman victory, however. As Publius returned to a hero's welcome, Camilla, the sister who had been betrothed to one of the Curiatii, caught sight of a mantle that she had made for her fiancé, which her brother had carelessly slung over his right shoulder as a trophy. The girl burst into tears and repeatedly struck her breast.

Publius was beside himself with rage. 'How dare you mourn an enemy of the Roman state!' he yelled. 'This is a moment of national rejoicing, and you want to turn it into a funeral. You're no sister of mine. You belong down in Hades with your lover. In fact, I'm sending you there right now. You deserve each other.'

So saying, he thrust his way through the crowd to where Camilla was lying on the ground, grief-stricken, and plunged his sword into her stomach.

The crowd gasped in horror. It was an intolerable and unnatural crime. Publius was immediately seized and brought before the king. Tullus was reluctant to pass a verdict on a man who was a popular hero, so he appointed a special tribunal known as the Duumvirs, the Two Men, to try the accused. After deliberation, the Two Men pronounced sentence.

PUBLIUS KILLS HIS SISTER CAMILLA

Publius kills his sister Camilla.

'You are to be blindfolded, hanged on a barren tree, and your corpse then scourged', one of the Two Men declared. 'Before we carry out the punishment, do you wish to lodge an appeal?'

'I do', Publius replied. 'I call upon my father to testify to my loyalty to the state.'

A messenger was duly dispatched to Horatius' house. After a lengthy hiatus the old man was brought before the court. He was leaning heavily on two canes and supported by a slave at each elbow.

'Noble Horatius', said one of the Two Men. 'Your son Publius has been found guilty of a heinous crime. Have you anything to say that might induce us to commute the death penalty which we have just passed?'

The old man glared at both Two Men.

'Anything that might induce you to commute the death penalty?' he snarled. 'Do you have any appreciation of what my son did today? This city would be subject to Alba Longa if it weren't for him. As for that accursed daughter of mine, I am glad she died a painful death. I disown her. My son has shown outstanding devotion to the public weal. You call yourselves judges? Take me home, slaves. I've nothing further to say to these quill-pushers, these time-servers, these nancy boys.'

The Two Men were in a very tight spot. They knew that, if they went ahead with the death sentence, there would be a popular uprising. At the same time they couldn't let Publius off scot-free. That would have set an extremely dangerous precedent, so they decided to make an example of him by subjecting him to a punishment heavy with symbolism. They placed a horizontal bar on top of two vertical bars some three feet high and made Publius stoop beneath it with his head covered.

'By bowing your head you show that you submit to the authority of the law', they declared. 'After that we permit you to go free. May every Roman learn from your example that no one is above the law.'

In later times, and in the perverse way that humans have of re-interpreting history, Publius' descendants have come to regard the punishment of subjugation that was meted out to their illustrious ancestor as a badge of pride. Every year they set up a yoke to commemorate Publius' service to the state and perform a religious ceremony in his honour.

This was not the end of the rivalry between Rome and Alba Longa. Far from it. Before long the Albans began to resent the fact that they had become subject to Rome merely because their champions had been narrowly defeated. They made their resentment known to Mettius Fufetius, who found himself under pressure to stage a revolt. His opportunity came when Tullus sought his help in a war against Fidenae, a city that lies some five miles north of Rome.

Mettius turned up to fight alongside the Romans as requested. However, just as their services were most needed, he gave the signal for his troops to withdraw. He was hoping that the Romans would be defeated as a result of his treachery. No such luck. They were victorious even without the assistance of the Albans.

After the battle, Tullus was furious. He arrested Mettius and addressed the Alban people as follows: 'Your king has acted treasonably. He has broken his solemn pledge of allegiance. That is unforgivable. Though you, his subjects, acted under his orders, I hold you guilty, since you followed him down the same treacherous path. Today I shall destroy Alba Longa as a warning to others who may be tempted to break their oath of loyalty to the Roman state. You'll all be transferred to Rome. I will grant you citizenship with the right to hold public office.'

Tullus turned to Mettius and said disdainfully, 'There are no words to describe my contempt for you. You are a man of divided loyalty – the most shameful type of man on the face of this earth. Your punishment is decorpitation, which in plain Latin means the separation of one or more limbs from your body. In your case, all your limbs.'

The king gave the order that Mettius be tied, spread-eagled, to a pair of chariots each drawn by a team of four horses facing in opposite directions. At his signal, two grooms raised their whips and struck both teams of horses. The horses leapt forward and Mettius was torn limb from limb. His screaming trunk was left to bleed out on the road, to the delight of dogs and buzzards and crows and various small animals that crept and crawled.

It's true that the Romans were a bloodthirsty people, but on no other occasion did they ever perform anything quite so abominable as this. They prided themselves on the clemency that they showed to conquered peoples, even though their conduct sometimes failed to measure up to their self-image.

The Albans were now forced to watch as their homes and temples were destroyed. Then, under guard, and in deepest dejection, they shuffled from the ruined city towards their new home while dogs howled. Such was the fate of the city that had been founded by Aeneas' son Ascanius.

Tullus Hostilius died soon afterwards, struck by a lightning bolt from Jupiter. He had made a serious *faux pas* while performing a new ritual in Jupiter's honour. No god, least of all Jupiter, takes an insult to his dignity lying down.

Chapter 8

An Immigrant Becomes King

Rome's fourth king was Ancus Marcius. Ancus fought a number of wars and founded the port of Ostia at the mouth of the River Tiber. There aren't any particularly interesting legends connected with him, so I will pass on to his successor, an Etruscan called Lucomo.

Lucomo's father had migrated to Etruria from Corinth in southern-central Greece to better himself and his family.

A word about the Etruscans. We don't know where they came from originally. They may have been a native Italic people or they may have been immigrants from Asia Minor/Turkey. Their territory, which lies to the north of Rome, roughly corresponded to modern-day Tuscany, the name of which derives from 'Etruscan'. There were twelve Etruscan cities in total, of whom the most important for our story were Veii, Caere and Clusium.

The Etruscans had a profound impact on Roman culture. They were extremely learned in the interpretation of the entrails of animals slain in sacrifice, a highly technical discipline known as haruspicy. If you want to know whether a course of action will turn out favourably, it's advisable to engage the services of a *haruspex*. The *haruspex* will examine a chicken's liver because that is the way the gods often choose to reveal the future. If the liver looks a bit dodgy, he'll obviously tell you to abandon the plan. The science is a bit more complicated than that – a lot, for instance, depends on the health of specific parts of the liver – but that's the general idea. Another feature of Etruscan culture is that their dead were very sanguinary, by which I mean they liked to drink blood.

At the time when Ancus Martius was on the throne, the Etruscans were a force to be reckoned with. They would remain a thorn in the side of the Romans for two hundred years. Theirs was a much more advanced civilization, and it was by no means a foregone conclusion that the wars the two peoples fought would end in Rome's favour.

Lucomo realised that no matter how hard he worked, he'd never be fully accepted in Etruscan society. This greatly troubled his wife

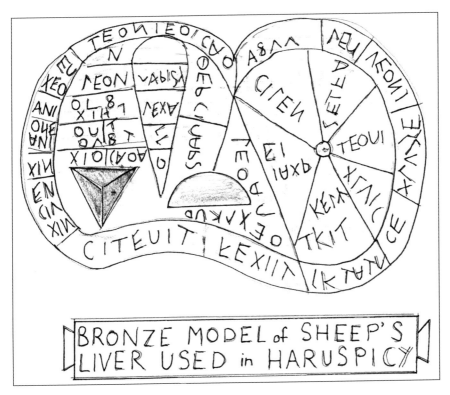

Model of a sheep's liver used in haruspicy.

Tanaquil, who was extremely ambitious. She decided that the only place where they would be able to thrive was in Rome. The Romans welcomed outsiders, irrespective of their background and circumstances. Numa had been a Sabine, and Ancus Marcius, the current king, was half-Sabine. There was no reason, she surmised, why the next king of Rome shouldn't be an Etruscan.

Accordingly they packed up their possessions and set off for Rome. Lucomo had inherited a fortune from his father's terracotta tile-manufacturing industry and they were confident they could flourish in the burgeoning new settlement that lay to the south.

Just as they were approaching the outskirts of the city, something extraordinary happened. A white-breasted eagle swooped down and snatched Lucomo's cap off his head with its ochre talons. The bird flew upwards, flapping its wings noisily and screeching. After circling around their cart, it swooped down again and neatly replaced the cap on Lucomo's head.

81

'It's a sign from Jupiter!' Tanaquil cried ecstatically, jumping up and down in the cart. 'It means you're highly favoured. You're going to achieve great things in Rome. I wouldn't be surprised if the crown didn't drop on your head just like your cap did just now.'

Though less given to outbursts of enthusiasm than his wife, Lucomo was also impressed. He discarded his name and introduced himself to the locals as Lucius Tarquinius Priscus, which obviously sounded much more Roman. 'Tarquinius' was a reference to his birthplace in Etruria, a town called Tarquinii.

Priscus, as I will now call him, soon became something of a celebrity. He was charismatic, enterprising and resourceful. Eager to move up the social ladder, he wined and dined the good and the great and used his fortune to acquire political influence.

Before long Ancus got to hear of Priscus and invited him to the *regia*.

'You look like an intelligent and responsible individual, Priscus', the king said after giving him the once-over. 'And I hear good things about you. Would you agree to be the guardian of my two sons? I need someone with a bit of backbone to keep them in line.'

'That's an unlooked-for honour, your majesty', Priscus replied deferentially. 'I'd be delighted of course.'

When he told Tanaquil of the offer, she was ecstatic.

'This is precisely the opportunity we've been waiting for!' she exclaimed, rubbing her hands together gleefully. 'Old Ancus is a doddery old fart. He's bound to kick the proverbial amphora soon, so cozy up to him now and then you'll be able to edge his sons out of the way.'

A year or two later Ancus fell and banged his head on the base of a column in the *regia*. Whether he slipped or whether he was pushed is a mystery. Either way, he died instantly. Priscus immediately summoned Ancus' two sons.

'This is a very sad occasion', he said meretriciously, idly picking a mosquito from his goblet of wine with one hand while wiping away a non-existent tear in affected grief with the other. 'You have my deepest condolences. Your father was very dear to me. Why don't you both go on a hunting expedition? An event like this shakes a fellow up. Take a breather. I'll hold the reins during your absence. No pun intended. Ha, ha, ha.'

The youths exchanged glances. They had never trusted Priscus.

Observing their suspicion, Priscus suddenly became businesslike. 'It's agreed then. You'll both leave the day after the funeral. Now, if you don't mind, I've got a lot of work to attend to, planning the event. I want it to be a magnificent affair.'

So saying, he waved them away and pretended to get back to studying the roll that was laid out on his desk.

As soon as Ancus' sons had left Rome, Priscus announced that he was holding an election for the kingship. Then he went about canvassing – knocking on doors and smiling for the ancient equivalent of a photo op. He was the first Roman ever to hold a political rally. There were no other candidates and he was duly elected Rome's fifth king. Tanaquil's prophecy had indeed come true.

A few years later a miraculous event occurred in the *regia* that took everyone who witnessed it by surprise. The head of a sleeping boy called Servius Tullius suddenly burst into flames for no evident reason. Everyone began screaming, whereupon Priscus and Tanaquil rushed into the room, anxious to discover what all the fuss was about. A slave was just about to empty a jug of water over the boy's head when Tanaquil abruptly restrained her.

'Don't!' she screamed. 'The shock will kill him. It's a sign from the gods.'

Once they were alone, Tanaquil stroked the child's golden brow and said to her husband, 'This boy is going to be the next king of Rome. We must do everything we can to protect him.'

Priscus was completely thrown off balance. 'What about our own sons?' he demanded. 'Shouldn't one of them be next?'

'Jupiter has spoken', Tanaquil announced flatly.

Priscus had unwavering faith in his wife's ability to interpret omens by this point, so he accepted her pronouncement and began grooming the lad to be his successor.

Servius' background is obscure, though his name would seem to testify to his servile origin. One explanation is that he was the son of a Latin princess named Ocrisia, who was captured in war. Due to a chronic shortage of eligible Roman *virgines intactae*, Ocrisia was appointed to the rank of Vestal Virgin. While tending the hearth, however, the negligent girl caused the juice of a sacrificial offering to extinguish the flame. Instantly a disembodied phallus or a delicate verisimilitude thereof – whether a phenomenon or a noumenon is impossible to say – impregnated her on or in the spot. Voilà. In due course she gave birth to a bouncing baby boy. Or so the story goes.

TANAQUIL and SERVIUS TULLIUS

Tanaquil and Servius Tullius.

'First a bloody immigrant robs us of the throne, and now a slave is about to do so!' the elder of Ancus' two sons exclaimed in white-hot fury. 'Are we going to allow this? We're the butt of ridicule. I say we kill Priscus immediately. We can deal with Servius later.'

'Sounds like a plan', the younger brother replied.

The boys hired the services of a pair of arrant knaves, who staged a pretend brawl outside the *regia*. Each knave was claiming the other had cheated him. Before long members of the palace staff came out to see what all the shouting was about. The knaves said they had come to the king to appeal for justice. The palace staff reported the matter to Priscus, who agreed to adjudicate the matter.

Once they had been admitted into the king's presence, the men continued to put up a show of arguing and insulting one another. Just at the moment when Priscus was appealing for calm, however, one of them whipped out an axe which he had concealed under his tunic and brought it down heavily on Priscus' head, splitting his skull neatly into two. Blood spilled everywhere.

A gasp of horror arose. Tanaquil, who was seated beside her husband, didn't miss a beat, however. She had the knaves arrested and put out a report that Priscus had only sustained a minor injury.

'If anyone breathes a word about this, I'll see they die a horrible death', she warned.

In the ensuing power vacuum Servius Tullius ascended the throne almost imperceptibly. No official announcement was made of Priscus' death. For the first time in Roman history, no election of a successor was held. It was, none the less, a smooth transition of power.

Many years passed. Servius did several notable things. He built a temple to Diana on the Aventine Hill and he divided the citizen body into five property classes with the wealthy having the largest share of the vote, even though they were the smallest demographic. Now it was the turn of the sons of Priscus and Tanaquil, Lucius and Arruns, to be irate. They were married to Servius' daughters, Tullia Major and Tullia Minor.

An aside. For some inexplicable reason the Romans never came up with the idea of giving personal names to their daughters. A daughter took the name of the *gens* or clan to which she belonged. A girl who belonged to the Julian gens, for instance, was called Julia, and a girl from the Claudian *gens* took the name Claudia. Tullia Major was therefore the elder daughter of Servius Tullius, and Tullia Minor was his younger daughter. If there had been a third daughter, she would have been called Tullia Minima. If Servius had had a fourth daughter, he would have had to rename them all, calling the eldest Tullia Maxima, the second eldest Tullia Major, the third eldest Tullia Minor, and the youngest Tullia Minima.

Tullia Minor was married to Arruns. Not to mince matters, Arruns lacked spunk. He was so destitute of spunk in fact that Tullia Minor, who had a plethora of the stuff herself, began flirting with his brother Lucius.

'What a pity we're both married to such losers', she said to Lucius one day when they were standing beside a fountain in the shape of the god Priapus that was concealed by blue hydrangeas. 'I don't know how you can bear my sister. She never has anything original to say. You and I have so much in common. Oh, if only you were my husband, I'd soon show you how we could shake things up here.'

She had planted the seed in Lucius' ear, where it duly came to fruition. Shortly afterwards a wheel fell off Arruns' chariot as he was speeding down the Appian Way, causing the vehicle to smash into one of the tombs at the side of the road. Then a few days later Tullia Major died in a boating accident.

Within the month Tullia Minor and Lucius had wed. Servius Tullius, who was now feeble and infirm, was unable to raise any objection.

Not to put too fine a point upon it, Tullia Minor was a monster. She lacked the least vestige of humanity and now began plotting to kill her father. She told her husband she wouldn't be able to rest until she had seen him crowned king.

'Your father was an immigrant, Lucius, and he managed to ascend the throne. What's holding you back? You've got all the qualities of leadership – use them in gods' names. More important, you've got me at your side. I don't intend to live my life as a slave to another man, even if that man happens to be my father. It's time to act. Servius is senile. He can hardly get dressed by himself. Now's the perfect time to grab the throne. If you don't, it'll be too late. I would rather die than be married to a man of no ambition. Your brother was a loser, and I had no patience for him. If you don't show some grit, I've had it with you too.'

On and on she went, day after day, till Lucius could stomach it no more.

'Very well, my dove of doves, my princess of myrrh', he said one evening when they were in bed together. 'You've convinced me. There's a meeting of the Senate tomorrow. I'm going to declare myself king. No messing.'

At the crack of dawn Lucius donned his toga and headed to the Senate house. To the astonishment of all those present, he seated himself in the curule throne, which was reserved exclusively for the king.

'Look here, conscript fathers', Lucius began, casting his eye warily around the chamber in case anyone thought of assassinating him. 'Things can't go on like this. Our king, bless his heart, is no longer fit to govern. He's neglecting the affairs of state. You've all noticed how he nods off in meetings. Important decisions are being constantly deferred. The state

Coin depicting the curule throne flanked by fasces.

totters. Rome needs a firm hand at the tiller. We're still hedged in on all sides by our enemies. They're itching to mount a campaign against us. Servius is of servile origin. I don't like to bring this up at this late point in his reign but it's time Rome had a king worthy of the name. No one has better credentials than I do. I think we'll all agree that my father, Lucius Tarquinius Priscus, was a great king. I plan on being a great king as well.'

Lucius was about to call a vote when the doors of the chamber were flung open and Servius staggered in, accompanied by his royal retinue.

He was in his nightgown, his hair awry, his cheeks still flushed from sleep.

'What do you think you're playing at, Lucius?' he demanded in a high-pitched, gravelly voice, snatching up in a vain attempt to make himself look dignified the hem of his imperial toga which one of the senators was standing on. 'How dare you sit on my throne! That counts as treason. Get up immediately! If you don't, I'll have you horsewhipped.'

'Oh you will, will you?' Lucius jeered. 'We'll see about that.'

At this he grabbed hold of Servius by the scruff of his neck, spun him around, and hauled him down the steps of the Senate House. It was a humiliating spectacle to watch, but none of the senators dared raise a finger in protest.

Once they were outside, a fight broke out, some people acclaiming Lucius as their king, others defending Servius. Servius managed to escape and fled towards a poor district known as the Subura. Just as he was hobbling towards the Esquiline Hill, however, two assassins whom Tullia had hired for this purpose pounced on him and threw him to the ground. They began kicking him in the head and stomach until there was no longer any life left in him.

Death of Servius Tullius.

Tullia had driven to the Senate in her carriage. She was exultant when she heard what her husband had done.

'Go home, dear', Lucius ordered hastily. 'The crowd could turn nasty at any moment.'

Tullia wasn't one to be ordered around, but on this occasion she obeyed. She told her driver to take the back streets home. Just as they were turning a corner, the driver saw Servius' lifeless corpse lying in the road. He hastily brought the horses to a halt. Tullia snatched the whip from his hand and flicked it with such force that they reared up and galloped over her father's body. Blood spattered the carriage and stained her dress.

The memory of that terrible act is preserved in the name of the street where it occurred – the Street of Crime.

Chapter 9

Tarquin the Proud

Now began the reign of Rome's seventh and last king, Lucius Tarquinius Superbus or Tarquin the Proud. The adjective *superbus* was hardly a compliment. People only muttered it behind his back. Pride isn't something to take pride in, after all.

Tarquin, as I shall call him, soon won a reputation for both brutality and paranoia. He had spies in every great household and carried out a purge of all those he suspected of bearing a grudge against him. He trusted no one except close family members. Everyone, he believed, was plotting against him, even his closest advisors. And in time, his suspicion became true.

One of the most famous legends connected with his reign is how Rome came to acquire the famous books of Sibylline prophecy. One day an emaciated old crone with rheumy eyes and arthritic hands knocked on the door of the *regia*. Tarquin didn't have much going on, so he agreed to admit her into his presence.

The old crone rocked from side to side as she shuffled forward into the throne room. Her hair was uncovered and hung down to her shoulders. Her eyes were lustrous but encircled with dark patches. She was labouring under the weight of a number of hefty rolls wound around wooden poles that terminated in elaborately carved ivory knobs.

'May the favour of the gods rain thick blessings upon you, mighty king!' she wheezed.

'Who are you?' Tarquin demanded sourly, ignoring the greeting and casting a characteristically malignant glance in her direction. He was slouched on his throne, one leg resting on an arm, idly swinging back and forth. Tullia was seated next to him, having her hair trimmed and coloured by an army of slaves.

'I am the Cumaean Sibyl', the old crone replied, bowing low.

Tarquin immediately sat bolt upright. 'This is a rare honour, reverend lady', he declared, flashing an insincere smile with his fastidiously

Tarquin the Proud.

wincing mouth. 'What brings you to these parts, if I may be so bold as to ask?'

'I have an offer to make to you. I have nine rolls of prophecy, which I think will prove useful in years to come. I'm here to sell them to you at a very reasonable price.'

'That's most generous. I could do with some prophecies right now. How much are you asking for them? I'm sure we can come to a mutually beneficial agreement.'

Coins hadn't been invented back then, or if they had they weren't in common use. Most exchanges were conducted by barter. At any rate, history does not record what exactly the Cumaean Sibyl demanded. All we know is that it was exorbitant.

'Are you out of your mind, old woman?' Tarquin expostulated, casting a dubious eye on the arachnid scribblings that graced the outer surface of the rolls and almost jumping out of his throne. 'You call that reasonable? I call it daylight robbery. All that for those mouldy old rolls? You must think I'm a blithering idiot.'

The old woman didn't reply. Instead, she extracted three of the rolls from the bundle she was holding and casually tossed them into the fire. Within seconds their ends were blackened, flames enveloped them, and the rolls disappeared in a puff of smoke.

Tarquin couldn't believe his eyes. 'I thought they were supposed to be valuable!' he snorted derisively. 'Well, now they aren't worth a thing. What in the name of the Heavenly Twins did you do that for?'

'OK, there are six remaining', the Sibyl said, ignoring his question. 'Now will you buy them?'

'How much do you want now?' he asked suspiciously.

The Cumaean Sibyl.

'It's the same price for six as it was for nine.'

Tarquin's eyes widened in disbelief. 'You're bonkers! Have you eaten of the insane root? Why in gods' names would I pay the same price for fewer?'

'I take it that's a no', the Sibyl replied, shrugging. Whereupon she extracted three more rolls and tossed them equally casually onto the fire.

'You have one last chance', she said, fixing him with a steely stare.

Tarquin was on the point of summoning a guard to eject her when Tullia suddenly grabbed him by the arm.

'Buy them,' she ordered.

'What?'

'I said buy them.'

'How much do you want for the remaining ones?' Tarquin asked, his voice barely audible.

'You know the price', the old woman replied quietly, dangling the remaining three rolls above the flames.

Tarquin shot a glance at Tullia. She nodded.

'OK', he said. 'I'll pay you.'

'A sensible decision', the Sibyl observed. 'It was your last chance to preserve the wisdom that had been handed down through the ages.'

And that is how Rome acquired the three books of Sibylline prophecy, which Tarquin placed under lock and key in the Temple of Jupiter Best and Greatest on the Capitoline Hill.

Years passed. One evening, just as he was about to retire for the night, Tarquin was horrified to see a serpent crawling out of a wooden column that supported the roof of the *regia*. Convinced this was a very bad omen, he decided to seek professional help. He could have enlisted the services of the Cumaean Sibyl, but the matter was of such magnitude that he decided to consult the Delphic Oracle, the foremost fountainhead of prophecy in the ancient world, sacred to Apollo of the silver bow.

Because of the sensitivity surrounding the mission, Tarquin decided to entrust it to his two sons, Arruns and Titus. (He had a third son called Sextus, who will become important later.) He also co-opted the services of a certain Lucius Junius Brutus, the son of his sister Tarquinia. Tarquin had murdered Brutus' brother, but since the young man showed not the slightest indication that he suspected the king of being the perpetrator, he naturally assumed he was a complete idiot. *Brutus* actually means 'numbskull' and that's what Tarquin believed him to be. Tarquin's motive

JUPITER BEST AND GREATEST

Jupiter Best and Greatest.

in including him on the mission to Delphi was to provide Arruns and Titus with some light relief. Delphi, I might point out, is 759 miles from Rome as the crow flies. Given the state of ships and of roads back then, virtually non-existent, the journey was going to take them six to eight weeks.

94

Brutus was nobody's fool, however. He had merely assumed the guise of an idiot to save his skin after his brother's murder. Fearing that his cousins might report him to their father if he abandoned this role, he laughed at their insults so as to give the impression that he had no idea that he was the butt of their humour.

Delphi is called the navel of the Earth because Jupiter once released two eagles in opposite directions to determine the exact centre of the world. This is the spot where they met. The Earth's navel is the source of all wisdom.

When the Romans arrived at the sanctuary, they found hundreds of petitioners awaiting to put a question to the Pythia, the priestess of Apollo. They had to stand in line for many hours before finally edging their way forward to the head of the queue.

When at long last they were ushered into the Temple of Apollo, they dimly discerned an old woman dressed in a long gown of nondescript colour, whom they took to be the Pythia. She was rocking back and forth, sitting cross-legged on a stone omphalus. An omphalus is a bullet-shaped object covered with criss-cross markings. It's supposed to represent a three-dimensional navel, if you can imagine such a thing.

'Reverend mistress, can you tell us how to interpret the portent of a snake emerging from a wooden column that supports the roof of a king's palace?' Arruns, who was the elder brother, inquired.

The Pythia fixed her beady eyes on him. 'You mean you've come all this way just to ask me this?' she demanded scornfully. 'Even an idiot can work that one out. It means the king's days are numbered.'

'Well, yes of course, I knew that', Arruns replied hurriedly, trying to save face. 'Even so, I'm grateful to have my suspicions confirmed. But here's the real question. Which of us will become king of Rome once the incumbent has passed away? Will it be me or my brother Titus here?'

'The next king of Rome will be the one who is the first to kiss his mother', the Pythia replied sonorously, her voice echoing in the temple's dark recesses.

'Thanks, Pythia', Arruns remarked, somewhat huffily. 'That's very helpful. We'll make a donation on the way out.'

Once they emerged into the daylight, Arruns said to Titus, 'We mustn't breathe a word of this to our brother Sextus. We don't want him cashing in on this. When we get back to Rome, I suggest we draw lots to determine who will kiss our mother first. Agreed?'

'Agreed.'

Just at that moment, Brutus, who was two steps behind and who had been listening intently to all that had transpired, gave a startled cry. The two brothers abruptly spun round to find him lying face down in a puddle.

'You clumsy idiot', Arruns remarked, bursting into laughter. 'We can't take you anywhere. You're a perfect disgrace. Keep your distance. I don't want you messing up my tunic with your dirty paws.'

Brutus had worked out that the Pythia was referring not to a biological mother but to Mother Earth, whom his lips had now kissed. However, he wisely decided to bide his time.

Lucius Junius Brutus.

Chapter 10

The Rape of Lucretia

Throughout these first centuries of their history, there was virtually no let-up in the wars that the Romans had to fight against their neighbours. One of their principal enemies during the reign of Tarquin the Proud were the Rutulians, whom Aeneas had fought centuries ago.

The Romans had established a camp outside Ardea, the capital city of the Rutulians, which lies about twenty miles south of Rome. To help pass the time when the action was slow, they used to play dice and gossip. One afternoon Tarquin's third son Sextus invited his mates over for a drink. Before long a heated argument was taking place as to whose wife was the most modest. *Pudicitia*, or modesty was a highly prized virtue among women in the eyes of the Romans. They expected their wives to stay at home and keep a low profile, especially when they were off on a military campaign, as was often the case.

Each of the young men present claimed that *his* wife deserved the prize for modesty. As the afternoon wore on into the evening, and the drink began to flow, things became more and more acrimonious. Eventually insults began to be hurled, and, just when it looked as if the company might come to blows, Lucius Tarquinius Collatinus, a relative of Sextus, made a suggestion.

'Calm down, gentlemen, calm down', he said. 'We're at war with the Rutulians, not with ourselves. There's only one sensible way to settle this. I suggest that we ride to Rome tonight – it'll take us less than an hour – and see what our wives are actually up to. I bet you anything my Lucretia will put all your wives in the shade.'

All agreed enthusiastically, each being eager to claim the prize which he saw as reflecting on his own honour. With one accord and without more ado they mounted their horses and galloped towards Rome. One by one each visited his home with the others as witnesses, to discover what his wife was up to in his absence.

'I didn't expect to see you here tonight, darling', the first wife whom they visited said, clearly taken aback. 'I hope you don't mind but I invited a few of my friends over for drinks. It gets so boring, sitting here alone night after night. Sorry about all the shouting. Hey, you lot. Can you keep the noise down? I can't hear a word my husband is saying.'

Everywhere the men went, it was the same old thing. Their wives were whooping it up without a care in the world, seemingly indifferent to the fact that their husbands were putting their lives in harm's way.

Finally, they visited Collatinus' house. Seated on the far side of the *impluvium*, in which rainwater collected into a sunken marble basin from a rectangular hole in the roof of the atrium, sat a demure young woman. She was diligently spinning by the light of a single candle. She wore a drab, ankle-length woollen dress tied at the waist by a simple cord. Apart from her face and hair, secured in a tight bun, only her toes were visible. Though she was dressed in unflattering attire, anyone could see she was a beauty. As soon as Collatinus entered, she gasped with pleasure, dropped her wool, and ran eagerly towards him.

'Lucius, darling!' she cried, wrapping her arms around him adoringly. 'I've been so worried about you. Does this mean the beastly war against the Rutulians is finally over?'

Collatinus turned to his friends. 'Gentlemen, this is my wife Lucretia. You see what a rare jewel I have?' Then, planting a chaste kiss on her forehead, he went on, 'Sadly, no, the war isn't over, my dear. My friends and I were in the area and decided we'd take a look at what our wives were up to in our absence.'

'Well, I'm not up to much, as you can see', Lucretia replied with a casual laugh, bringing his right hand to her lips and kissing it.

Collatinus' companions were bowled over by the young woman before them, but none more so than Sextus Tarquinius, who, like a malignant thief, was instantly consumed by an ungovernable desire to possess her. In the days that followed, he was incapable of thinking of anything else but how to gain admittance into Collatinus' house. He fantasised constantly about how to satisfy his lust.

Eventually he hit on a plan. He waited till a severe thunderstorm occurred. Then he saddled his horse and galloped towards Rome. He arrived at Collatinus' house just as the storm was at its height. Bedraggled and caked in mud, his hair sopping wet, he banged on the door. When it opened, he gave his name to the doorkeeper, a handsome bronze-skinned Ethiopian, and was admitted into Lucretia's presence.

A ROMAN ATRIUM

A Roman atrium.

'I'm so sorry to appear unannounced', Sextus said, affecting an air of abject humility. 'I'm back in Rome to give my father an update on the course of the war. I just happened to be passing your house on foot – my horse stumbled on a pothole a few minutes ago – I must tell my father to alert the municipal workers to it – it's a hazard to man and beast, especially at night – and I was hoping you might not take offence if I sheltered in your vestibule for a few minutes till the worst of it passes. I do hope I'm not imposing. It's a foul night. I should have postponed my mission, but, well, my father wants to make sure that the army has all the supplies that it needs. Please forgive me for my presumptuousness.'

'Presumptuousness? You're not in the least presumptuous!' Lucretia exclaimed, rising to greet him. 'I'd have been offended if you *hadn't* stopped by. You poor man! No one, least of all a dear friend of my husband, should be out on a night like this. Here, let me take your tunic. It's soaked through. I won't have you standing there shivering. Come and warm yourself by the hearth. You must be frozen. And by the way, my name is Lucretia.'

'Thank you, Lucretia', Sextus replied. 'You're most kind.'

He crouched on the ground and began energetically rubbing his hands together over the flames of the hearth, while his teeth chattered.

'That was a funny prank you and my husband played on their wives the other evening', Lucretia observed, smiling. 'I heard you were testing us. Is that true? I feel sure your wife passed with flying colours. I hope I did. How's my Lucius? How's the war going? What's the latest report?'

'Lucius sends his love to you. He talks about you so much. He's doing fine. He offered to come with me but I knew it was going to be a beastly night, so I told him I'd go alone. The war's going extremely well, I'm happy to say. With any luck we should have those damned Rutulians on the ropes by the time of the Saturnalia.'

'That's great news! Do make yourself comfortable, dear man. Here, let me help you off with your boots. Then you can warm your feet.'

Turning to an elderly slave dressed in a brown smock, Lucretia said, 'Myrta, prepare dinner for our honoured guest. Oh, and heat up some mulled wine while you're at it.'

After the old woman had hobbled off, she said, 'You must stay for the night, Sextus. There's no point going out again. You'll catch a dreadful cold.'

'That's very kind of you, but I really think I should be getting back', Sextus replied, pretending to stifle a sneeze.

'I won't take no for an answer', Lucretia said peremptorily, wagging her index finger at him in a playful manner. 'In fact I order you to stay.'

'Well, in that case you make it very difficult for me. How can I possibly disobey an order from a lady?'

'You can't. I'd have to report you to your superior officer.'

The two of them laughed.

'I suppose the army could dispense with my services for just one night', Sextus said thoughtfully.

'Of course it can', Lucretia replied. 'Lucius would never forgive me if I let you go out again.'

Just then Myrta arrived with the dinner, which she placed before their guest on a side table.

'Make yourself comfortable', Lucretia said, indicating a chair.

Lucretia, it turned out, was quite a chatterbox, so the two of them spent the next hour amiably exchanging gossip about friends they had in common. It was clear to Sextus that she spent most of her time alone and was all too happy to have someone to talk to. He for his part took great care not to say anything that could possibly awaken her suspicions. Even so, he found it almost impossible to keep his eyes off her, observing the outline of the *strophium* that encased her *embonpoint*, and once or twice she caught him staring at her, whereupon he quickly averted his eyes. She put this down to his fatigue, however.

Eventually it was time to retire for the night.

'I trust you will get a good night's sleep after all your exertions', Lucretia said as they parted, her cheeks dimpling, extending her hand.

'Something tells me sleep won't be a problem', Sextus remarked. He took her hand and kissed it, while gazing up at her translucent lips.

Myrta showed him to his room. She placed beside his bed a little terracotta lamp with a rope wick burning in olive oil.

Sextus waited impatiently till the moment when he guessed all the household was fast asleep. Then, balancing his lamp in his hand, he stole along the corridor to Lucretia's bedroom. He cracked the door open and crept over to her bed. After setting the lamp on the tiled floor, he put one hand over her mouth and tightly squeezed her right breast with the other.

Lucretia tried to struggle but he placed his knee on her chest so that she could scarcely breathe. All she could produce was a muffled cry.

'Stay perfectly quiet', he hissed, putting his mouth close to her ear and licking her lobe. 'See this knife? If you utter a sound, I'll kill you. But if you submit to my will, I'll be out of here before you know it. No one will know anything about this.'

Lucretia, however, proved more than a match for her assailant. She used all her resources to resist by biting, scratching and kicking. Eventually he was forced to give up.

'OK, if you don't yield to my desire, I'll tell you what's going to happen', he said grasping her by the neck and almost choking her. 'First, I'll rape you, then I'll kill you. After that I'll slit the throat of

The rape of Lucretia.

that Ethiopian of yours and place him, naked, in your bed. I'll wake the whole household and tell everyone that I heard noises coming from your bedroom. I'll say that I ran to your rescue only to find you making passionate love to a slave, and that I was so disgusted by what I saw that I killed both of you out of my deep loyalty to your husband. Do you think anyone will doubt me? Your precious honour will be stained forever, and you'll have died for no reason. Is that what you want?'

When she heard these words, Lucretia ceased to put up any resistance. She lay still and let Sextus have his way with her. After he had satisfied his lust, which he did within a matter of minutes, he quickly dressed, left the house and galloped off. He took pride in the fact that he had outsmarted his victim. The storm had ended and the stars were shining brightly. When he rode back into the camp, he didn't have a care in the world.

Lucretia was not the kind of woman to take what had happened lying down, however. As soon as Sextus left, she picked up a quill and with a trembling hand wrote to her husband, urging him to come to her with a trusted friend. She sealed the letter and sent for a messenger.

She had made no mention of the rape but her tone of urgency, coupled with the shakiness of the handwriting, made Collatinus fear the worst as he read the letter later that day. His closest friend happened to be Lucius Junius Brutus, whom he invited to accompany him. Brutus readily agreed. The two men arrived in Rome just as Phoebus was mounting his chariot the next morning.

'Lucretia, it's me!' Collatinus shouted, as he ran down the vestibule into the atrium. On entering, however, he stopped dead in his tracks. His wife was huddled up on the floor, shivering feverishly and moaning. Her upper lip was swollen, one of her cheeks was scarred, and both her eyes were blackened and bloodshot. Myrta was beside her, doing her best to comfort her mistress.

'In the name of Juno, protector of all married women, tell me who has done this terrible thing to you?' Collatinus cried. He gently raised his wife to her feet and sat her down in a chair. Turning to Brutus, he said, 'I think you should leave us alone for a few minutes.'

'No, don't send your friend away', Lucretia said agitatedly. 'I want both of you to hear this. I want there to be a witness. Last night a man whom you know raped me. A man whom you trusted. He did it in this house – in our bedroom. I couldn't resist. He told me that, if I did, he would make it seem as if I was having an affair with one of our slaves.'

'Who was it?' Collatinus demanded in a hoarse whisper. 'Whoever is guilty of this foul crime, I swear by Jupiter Best and Greatest he will pay for what he has done.'

Lucretia clutched her husband by the arm. 'My rapist was the king's son, your commander, Sextus Tarquinius. Sextus gained access by pretending to seek shelter from the storm. He is not only guilty of the foulest crime in raping me, but he has also violated the sacred bond of hospitality between guest and host. And because of his deception and violence, I am dishonoured forever. I will never live down the insult to my honour.'

'That's simply not true, Lucretia', Collatinus protested vehemently. 'The monster left you no choice. If you hadn't submitted, he would have killed you and your death would have proven your guilt.'

'That's beside the point', Lucretia remarked. 'People will say that I put my safety above my family's honour –'

'Not so, my beloved, most devoted wife! I'll swear before the world that you're innocent of any infidelity!'

'Let me finish, Lucius. No one will believe you. He's right about that. And that's not the worst of it. Wives in the future will say Lucretia dishonoured her family name and got away with it, so why shouldn't they do the same thing? They'll use my name to justify adultery. Is that what you want? To be regarded for all time as a cuckold? My mind is made up. Never will I allow any woman to use my name to excuse her unchaste behaviour.'

At this Lucretia suddenly produced a small knife from the folds of her dress and plunged it deep into her stomach.

Collatinus and Brutus tried desperately to staunch the blood, but Lucretia had struck home. Within seconds her eyes grew misty and closed in death. Then her limbs became slack.

Brutus laid a firm hand on his friend's shoulder. 'I promise you that your wife has not died in vain', he said solemnly. 'She will be the catalyst for change. Her death has liberated us. I will see that Rome is rid of Tarquin the Proud and all his foul stock. We will be a free people from now on. Never again will Rome submit to tyrannical rule. This I swear in the name of the purest woman who has ever lived.'

Like everyone else, Collatinus had always thought that Brutus was something of an idiot. Now, however, he saw what mettle the man exhibited. He was astonished at the sudden transformation.

'There's no time to lose', Brutus continued, ignoring the look of amazement on his friend's face. 'We will display your wife's body in the Forum. I'll deliver an eloquent speech, explaining how she gave her life to defend the highest standards of womanly behaviour. Then I'll instance all the outrageous crimes committed by Tarquin and his accursed family. No woman will be honoured more highly than your beloved Lucretia. She will become an example to all women in the future.'

Collatinus' slaves bore Lucretia's body into the Forum and placed it on top of the Rostra, where speeches are delivered. A crowd soon began to gather, curious at first but later horrified when they observed the bloodstained corpse of a woman.

'ΑΜΕΙΝΟΝ
'ΑΠΟΘΝΗΣΚΕΙΝ
'Η 'ΑΙΣΧΡΩΣ
ΖΗΝ

⟨THE SUICIDE OF LUCRETIA⟩

The suicide of Lucretia (after Marcantonio Raimondi).

Brutus delivered a powerful indictment of Tarquin and his family. He ended by declaring that it was time for Rome to rid itself of the hateful institution of monarchy. His words carried the day and at the end of his speech he put forward a proposal to exile the Tarquins. A vote took place and a resolution to that effect was passed.

Fortified by the will of the people, Brutus headed directly to the camp outside Ardea, intent on gaining the support of the military. Tarquin, meanwhile, who happened to be away from Rome at the time, quickly caught wind that a rebellion was underfoot. He headed back to the city, eager to take refuge inside. When he arrived, however, he found his family sheltering outside the walls. They informed him that they were exiles.

Coin depicting the Temple of Jupiter Best and Greatest.

Tarquin was without doubt a cruel tyrant fully deserving of the adjective *superbus* but there were a few good things that he did for Rome. He made alliances with a number of Latin towns. He signed a treaty with Carthage. He supervised the construction of the *cloaca maxima*, the Great Drain, which runs through the Forum.

It wasn't his fault that it needs constant overhaul. Romans produce mountains of excrement every day.

Last but not least, he built the Temple of Jupiter Best and Greatest, Rome's premier temple, on top of the Capitoline Hill. Legend has it that when workers were digging its foundations they uncovered a human head, *caput* in Latin, indicating that Rome would one day be head of the world. Hence the origin of the name 'Capitol'. Each year a nail is banged into the wall of the temple as a way of averting plague. It was by counting these nails that the Romans were able to establish the date that the temple was founded – 509 – the year we have reached in our narrative.

Chapter 11

Brutus Becomes Consul

Tarquin decided that the safest place to go was Etruria since he enjoyed good relations with one of its kings, a certain Lars Porsena, who ruled over Clusium. Clusium is about a hundred miles north of Rome and the journey took the Tarquins several days.

'By Jove!' expostulated Lars Porsena, shocked by the bedraggled condition of his guests when they were ushered into his throne room. 'What in the name of that is holy has happened? You look a mess. This isn't the way a king should travel.'

'I need your help, Lars', Tarquin replied. 'I've been kicked out of Rome by some insurgents. I wouldn't be surprised if you don't end up in the same boat. Anti-monarchical sentiment could easily spread to Clusium. These are dangerous times. You need to nip it in the bud right now. Plus – don't forget this – I'm an Etruscan by ancestry, so we're actually kinsmen and I deserve your support. The Romans always held my Etruscan origins against me. They'd like nothing better than to wipe Etruria from the face of the earth.'

Lars was silent a long time, scratching his bristly chin, as was his wont whenever he was thinking hard.

'All right, Lucius. I'll give you my support. I've never liked Romans anyway. Filthy upstarts, present company excepted. They're getting too big for their boots. There was bound to be a showdown sooner or later. This could be a win-win situation.'

Meanwhile, back in Rome, Brutus and Collatinus were hailed as liberators. It was they who now established the Republic, the *res publica*, a phrase which literally means 'common wealth'. The Republic was placed under the authority of annually elected magistrates, chief of whom are two consuls. Consuls have much of the authority previously invested in the king with these two important limitations: they hold office for only one year and each has the right of veto over the other's initiatives. In the first year of the Republic, Brutus and Collatinus were elected consuls without opposition.

Most people were ecstatic that Rome had finally rid itself of a hateful tyranny but there were some malcontents. Monarchy still had its supporters, particularly among the aristocracy, who had enjoyed ready access to the king and been able to sway his opinion in their favour. Now, under the new dispensation, they were no better than the rabble. In addition, a lot of people complained that Rome was still under the thumb of the Tarquins since Collatinus, whose full name was Lucius Tarquinius Collatinus, was a relative of the exiled king. It was a name of ill omen, they argued, indissolubly tied to tyranny.

Collatinus was a mild-mannered man and he certainly had no ambitions to re-instate the monarchy. Why would he? It was the crime against his wife that had brought about the overthrow of kingship. That should have bought him general goodwill.

What tipped the scales against him, however, was the fact that Brutus joined the ranks of his detractors. Although there's no evidence to suggest that Brutus was acting out of any desire to make a power grab, we cannot entirely rule that out. He now abandoned his friend and summoned an assembly in the Campus Martius or Field of Mars, which lies to the north of the Capitoline Hill.

'Collatinus, old chap', Brutus said genially, 'which of us here today does not appreciate the invaluable part that you played in the expulsion of the Tarquins? Let me be the first to express my deep appreciation for your service to our country. As we both know, however, service never ends and there is one more act of goodwill that I must ask you to perform. It is hardly surprising that the Roman people fear the return of the exiled tyrant. Though your loyalty to the Republic is unquestioned, the unfortunate fact is that you bear the hated name of the hated tyrant. So long as there remains in our midst a man who is related, however distantly, to that abhorred tyrant, our fellow countrymen will not sleep easily in their beds. I therefore call upon you, in the name of our forebear Aeneas, himself a refugee, to take yourself into exile, for the good of our newly established Republic – the Republic of which you are a founding father.'

Collatinus was dumbstruck. You could have knocked him down with a peacock's feather. He never suspected that Brutus would seek to get rid of him. They had endured so many trials together.

'You will, of course, retain possession of your property', Brutus continued in an ingratiating tone, 'but it is in the interests of all concerned that you remove yourself from the city within three days. This isn't, let me emphasise, an *ad hominem* expulsion. It's got nothing to do with you personally. All those bearing the name of Tarquin will be asked to leave. It goes without saying that your exile will be voluntary, but if you, ahem, fail to comply, steps will have to be taken. Let me just add that I regret deeply having to propose this action. I hope you can see that there is no other option. The safety of the Republic is my top priority.'

Collatinus was in no doubt that his life was now in danger. He left Rome the same day. An election to fulfil the vacant consulship was held soon afterwards and an aristocrat by the name of Publius Valerius was sworn in. Publius had played a leading part in the overthrow of the monarchy.

Brutus was right in one regard. The atmosphere in Rome was extremely tense. Two of the chief trouble-makers were his sons Titus and Tiberius.

'Between you and me, I think it's a shame that Tarquin was exiled', Titus said, while he and Tiberius were dining with some aristocratic friends. 'Let's admit it. Life used to be damn good when he was in charge. Now we have to do what we're told. I admit that Tarquin made the odd mistake – who doesn't? – we're all human – but, all things considered, Rome prospered under his rule. Now the city is at the mercy of the mob. What qualifications does a mob have for determining who is fitted to lead us? Besides, how can there be any continuity if our leaders are chopping and changing from one year to the next? It stands to reason that the Republic is a recipe for disaster.' Titus leant forward and dropped his voice. 'Listen, fellows, I've got an idea. Why don't we sound out Tarquin and see if he can lean on Lars Porsena to make an assault on Rome with a view to re-instating him? I say we write him a letter now.'

It didn't take much to get them all to agree. Titus dictated a letter to one of his slaves, which they all signed. It so happened, however, that the slave was in the pay of the consuls, to whom he promptly brought the letter, thereby providing proof of their criminal intent.

Brutus and Valerius had no choice. They ordered the immediate arrest of the conspirators, all of whom, including Brutus' sons, were aristocrats in their late teens or early twenties. They were brought to trial and found guilty of treason. Treason carried the death penalty, which the consuls pronounced solemnly.

The condemned were immediately hauled off. A large crowd had assembled to witness their punishment. Brutus and Valerius took their seats on the tribunal in the Forum. In their joint names they ordered the prisoners to be stripped, tied to stakes, and flogged mercilessly. As they lay lifeless on the ground, Brutus signalled to a slave, who stepped forward and severed their heads from their bodies.

'Throw them in the common pit', Brutus said. Then he rose and departed.

Throughout this heart-rending ceremony Brutus displayed not a trace of emotion. Not a tear dropped from his eyes. No indication of the pain he must have been feeling clouded his brow. Whatever one may think of him, he deserves credit for the stoical way in which he conducted himself on that day. No father has ever had to witness a more chilling sight.

The slave informer was rewarded for service to the state by being granted his freedom and awarded Roman citizenship. Legend has it that he was the first Roman slave ever to be freed. The ceremony that established his new status was known as 'manumission', a word which derives from the Latin verb *manumitto* meaning 'I dismiss with my hand'.

When Tarquin learned how his supporters had been treated, he was furious. He made the rounds of the Etruscan cities and was able to prevail upon the people of Tarquinii, his ancestral home, and of Veii, Rome's inveterate foe, to join forces with him.

The Etruscan army crossed the frontier and headed towards Rome, where they were met by an opposing army. At the head was Brutus, dressed in his consular armour. When Tarquin's son Arruns saw him, he became enraged.

'How dare you drive my father from the throne?' he bawled. 'Look at you, dressed in all the trappings of power that you usurped from him. You're just a swaggering numbskull. Brutus by name and Brutus by nature. May the immortal gods assist me in exacting revenge for the insult you have inflicted on our family honour.'

Arruns dug his heels into his horse and charged towards Brutus. A bitter fight ensued. Eventually Arruns thrust his sword into Brutus' midriff, but at the exact same moment Brutus thrust his sword into Arruns' stomach. Both men fell from their horses and gasped their last.

The battle raged for many more hours. When darkness called a halt to the fighting, there was no clear victor on either side. Both armies had sustained heavy casualties. It was left to the gods to decide who had won. In the silence of the night the voice of Silvanus, god of the woods, was heard declaring that the Romans had won. Silvanus had counted the number of dead on both sides and by his exact calculation the Romans had sustained one fewer casualty than the Etruscans. The Etruscans submitted to Silvanus' verdict with a good grace – who would challenge a god to a counting contest? – and when the sparks from Phoebus' chariot began to illuminate the sky next morning there was not a single Etruscan soldier to be seen.

Brutus' body was borne back to Rome, where he was honoured with a state funeral on a scale that had never been witnessed before. Women were especially demonstrative in their lamentations, in recognition of the fact that he had championed the cause of Lucretia.

Chapter 12

Horatius Defends the Bridge

Despite the recent victory over the Etruscans, the Republic remained on edge. There just wasn't enough food to go around and the poor were beginning to starve. The Senate knew that if this state of affairs continued, a wave of nostalgia for the Tarquins would eventually take over. The Republic was still in its infancy, and it was entirely possible that tyranny might raise its ugly head again.

To make matters worse, resentment was building against the surviving consul, Publius Valerius. This was mainly due to the fact that he hadn't authorised an election to appoint a replacement for Brutus. A rumour thus begun to circulate that Publius was aiming at monarchy. This suspicion was fuelled by the fact that he had begun building a huge villa on top of the Velian Hill. His purpose, so his detractors claimed, was to establish himself in a position of dominance and thus spy on the populace below. This all goes to show how insecure the Romans felt at this date and how fragile their constitution was.

Valerius, however, had no such intentions. Once the rumour that he was harbouring political ambitions reached him, he determined to scotch it once and for all. He called a meeting of the assembly and ostentatiously ordered his attendants, known as lictors, to lower their *fasces*. *Fasces*, from which our word 'fascism' derives, are bundles of rods with an axe at the centre. They symbolise a magistrate's jurisdiction and power. The rods signify his power to beat any offender and the axe signifies his power to execute. By ordering his lictors to lower them, he was divesting himself of his authority.

'I deeply regret that some of you are of the opinion that I have been seeking to re-introduce a monarchy', he declared. 'I never meant to cause any offence and I would never betray the Republic. Sole power is as unacceptable to me as it is to you. Rome will never revert to kingship again. However, I understand that perceptions are all-important and I take responsibility for the suspicions that I have inadvertently aroused.

113

Since the villa that I was building on the Velian Hill has given rise to concern, I've given orders for it to be destroyed. Instead I shall build my modest home at the bottom of the hill. I hope this will allay your fears. I further propose that any Roman who in the future even so much as mentions that he would like to see a return to monarchy be deprived of his citizenship and sent into exile.'

Everybody clapped when they heard these words. Valerius was accorded the nickname Publicola, which roughly translates 'Friend of the People'. It was the name that Alexander Hamilton, author of many of *The Federalist Papers*, assumed as his pseudonym during the American Revolutionary War. He did so in deference to the fact that Valerius had taken a leading role in establishing the Republic on a secure basis.

No sooner had Valerius put the minds of the populace at rest, however, when another crisis arose. Word reached Rome that Lars Porsena, with Tarquin in tow, was preparing an assault on the city. All of a dither, the senators held an emergency meeting.

'What in the name of Castor and Pollux are we to do?' asked the first speaker, wringing his hands in despair. 'Our army is no match for that of Lars Porsena. It would be wiped out if it met him in the field.'

'It's obvious. We have to destroy the bridge', said the second speaker. 'We don't want the Etruscans waltzing into Rome. If we destroy the bridge, at least we'll be able to prepare for a siege.'

Back in those days there was only one bridge over the Tiber. It was known as the *Pons Sublicius* or Sublician Bridge because of its *sublicae* or wooden supports. It was barely wide enough to permit two carts to cross in opposite directions.

'There's only one problem with that strategy', said the third speaker. 'It will leave all the people who live on the Janiculum totally exposed. We have to organise an emergency evacuation from the villages on the other side of the river. Only after the evacuation has been completed can we start to demolish the bridge. We cannot abandon our fellow citizens.'

The Janiculum is the hill that lies to the west of the Tiber. Though fortified by a low wall, it was far more vulnerable than Rome. It was named after Janus, the two-faced god of beginnings and endings.

'Agreed', said a fourth. 'We also need to organise a demolition squad to saw through the bridge's *sublicae* immediately after the evacuation has been completed.'

'Exactly, except that any evacuation is a lengthy undertaking', pointed out a fifth. 'We'll be lucky to complete it before the Etruscans are here, and even if we do, I doubt the demolition squad will have enough time to destroy the bridge. Suggestions, anyone?'

At that moment an aristocrat named Horatius Cocles promptly stepped forward. Horatius belonged to the same patrician family as the Horatii triplets who had saved Rome centuries ago.

'I'll hold off the Etruscans at the far side of the bridge while the demolition team is doing its work', he declared. 'I just need two volunteers to help. That's all it will take to prevent the enemy from crossing. Who's up for the challenge?'

Two young men, named Spurius and Titus, smartly stood up.

'We're with you, Cocles old chap', said Spurius.

'One hundred per cent', said Titus.

A resolution was proposed, a vote was taken, and the plan implemented. Criers, men noted for their stentorian voices, were sent to every village in the Janiculum and beyond, ordering the residents to head to Rome immediately. It wasn't a moment too soon. Just as the last few stragglers were being herded across the bridge, the Etruscan army appeared on the horizon. There was nothing to prevent their advance. The army had taken refuge inside the city, along with the evacuees.

Horatius took up his position on the bridge and ordered his two comrades to stand on either side of him.

'Right, left, right, left', or in Latin '*Dex, sin, dex, sin*', he barked, since the Romans consider it unlucky to start off with the left foot. *Dex* is short for *dextra* and *sin* short for *sinistra*.

By the time they reached the far side of the bridge, the Etruscans were only a few hundred yards away.

'Ye gods!' Lars exclaimed, when he espied Horatius and his comrades blocking his advance, their swords drawn. 'Is this a suicide mission or what? Do these idiots think they can hold us off?'

His soldiers were equally amazed. They were tempted to jeer, but something told them that they might be facing more resistance than they were expecting.

Horatius, spying Tarquin in the ranks of the enemy, said to his comrades, 'You see that scumbag over there? He's the reason why we're putting our lives at risk. Are we going to let a traitor back into our city so that our wives and daughters can feed the lust of his sons?'

At this, all three men let out a battle cry that struck fear in the front rank of the Etruscan army.

Lars gave the order to charge but as his army scrambled forward, they created a bottleneck. Pushed forward by their comrades from behind, many Etruscans either fell into the river or were crushed to death, while those who made it to the head of the line were hacked down by Horatius and his comrades. Meanwhile, a team of experts was furiously sawing its way through the wooden posts of the bridge. Eventually a loud creak as of a creature in pain was heard.

'Get off the bridge now!' the sawyers called up.

'Do as they say!' Horatius yelled to Titus and Spurius. 'That's an order. I'll join you later.'

Titus and Spurius exchanged glances. They were about to protest but realised it would do no good. They both bolted across the bridge, followed by the demolition squad.

For a moment the Etruscans held back, awed by Horatius' courage. Then three of them stepped forward and charged at him. One of them

Horatius and the bridge.

succeeded in wounding Horatius in the thigh. He was about to move in for the kill when the bridge suddenly collapsed. The three Etruscans tumbled into the river and were quickly borne downstream by the swift current, their heads bobbing up and down briefly before they sank, never to be seen again.

Horatius plunged into the river head first.

The cry of triumph that had issued from the Romans was now tempered by concern for Horatius. For what seemed an eternity they scanned the surface, fearing the worst.

Meanwhile, in the river's depths, Horatius prayed to the River Tiber to give him the strength to swim ashore.

'If I have served Rome well today, Father Tiber, please come to my rescue.'

At this, the old river god swiftly emerged from his underwater grotto and swam to Horatius' rescue. Cradling his head in his arm, Tiber bore him gently to the surface and shielded him from the hail of missiles that the Etruscans rained down from the opposite bank.

Eventually Horatius gained the shore and clambered to safety, assisted by Spurius and Titus. An almighty cheer arose on the Roman side. Three men had held off an entire army – an unprecedented feat in the annals of warfare.

Chapter 13

Lars Porsena Learns a Thing or Two About the Romans

Horatius had saved Rome but the Etruscans had achieved their objective. The city was under siege and its population was locked inside the walls. Many of the Roman youth regarded this as a deep insult but no one more so than a certain Lucius Mucius. Mucius took the siege as a personal insult. He resolved to free Rome by assassinating Lars Porsena. It was a madcap idea, of course, but such was his fury and hatred for the Etruscans that he was prepared to risk life and limb. He knew, however, that if he slipped out of Rome without first notifying the Senate, he was likely to be arrested and executed as a deserter, so he took the sensible precaution of alerting that body to his plan.

'I doubt you'll get anywhere near the king, but we won't stop you', was the general verdict. 'Good luck, matey. You'll certainly need it.'

That same night, just when shadows were beginning to fill the hollows of the Alban Hills, Mucius left the city by one of its postern gates. He made his way upriver to a spot where he could swim across without being seen and then headed towards the Etruscan camp. He arrived around the first watch and spent the rest of the night hidden in a thicket, not far from where guards were posted. Next morning, his heart in his mouth, he bathed in a nearby stream and entered the camp as nonchalantly as he could. He knew a few words of Etruscan and was able to mingle among the soldiery without attracting any suspicion.

As luck would have it, Lars Porsena had summoned a meeting to beef up morale, so all attention was now focussed on the king. He gave a long rambling speech, in the course of which Mucius gradually inched his way to the front. He got there just after the king had finished talking. He had a sharp knife concealed under his tunic and was poised to execute his plan. The only problem was that he didn't actually know what Lars Porsena looked like. Two men dressed in decorated robes were standing on a low platform. Both looked august. One was holding a sceptre, the other a staff inlaid with gold filigree. It was impossible to determine who was the king. If he asked anyone, he'd obviously attract suspicion and be arrested. There was nothing to do but flick a mental coin, which is what he did.

Mucius broke through the crowd, rushed onto the platform, and plunged his dagger into the heart of the man holding the staff.

Instantly guards stepped forward and knocked him to the ground. After kicking him savagely in the head and then in the privates, they dragged him to his feet and presented him to the king. He had killed the wrong man.

Lars stared hard at Mucius. 'Before I order your execution, young man', he said, 'I want to know who you are and why you attempted such a rash deed? Are all Romans as stupid as you?'

Mucius was breathing with difficulty but he fixed Lars with a steely stare. He now delivered what has become one of the most famous pronouncements in Roman history.

'My name is Lucius Mucius', the youth declared. 'I am a Roman citizen. It is the nature of a Roman both to endure and to inflict hardship. Kill me by all means. But be warned that thousands like myself are standing ready to follow in my footsteps. You are destined to live the rest of your life in fear and trembling, never knowing when a dagger will pierce your heart. You will never defeat us.'

Lars Porsena was furious – but also impressed. He saw no reason to doubt what Mucius had said and suspected that numerous assassins were indeed queuing up to take him down.

'Tell me the names of your co-conspirators!' he shouted in a fury. 'If you don't, I'll burn you alive!'

Mucius maintained the same steely stare and remained tight-lipped.

'Very well, burn him!' Lars roared. 'I want the smell of his burning flesh to fill my nostrils.'

The guards fetched a stake and planted it in the ground. Then they proceeded to place logs around its base. Mucius was bound tightly to a stake from his waist downwards.

'This is your last chance', Lars snarled. 'What are their names?'

Mucius remained mute.

'Still nothing to say? OK, light the fire. See that it burns slowly so that his cries last a very long time.'

A guard jumped forward and lit some twigs, whose crepitations could soon be heard. Before long wisps of smoke were eddying around the prisoner's feet. Moments later flames were lapping around his body. It was now that Mucius finally broke his silence.

'I care nothing for my body', he cried out defiantly. 'All that matters to me is my service to the Roman state. I willingly sacrifice my life for the public good.'

Then, to the astonishment of all present, he extended his right arm and plunged it without flinching into the flames. Though he winced slightly as his arm reddened, no sound escaped his lips.

Lars was deeply moved. He was not one to inflict senseless cruelty on another human being. He ordered his guards to untie the youth and bandage up what remained of his charred arm.

'You are without doubt the most courageous – and frankly the most stupid – young man I have ever met', he said in a tone of grudging respect. 'You've done more harm to yourself than you have to me today. In return, I grant you your liberty. You're free to return to Rome. I hope that will teach you and your compatriots that the Etruscans hold courage in the highest esteem.'

You might think that Mucius would have displayed some gratitude for the king's generosity. Well, he didn't. Not in the least. He still had one more trick up his sleeve, if you'll pardon the somewhat unfortunate expression.

'I would never have divulged what I am about to say to you under torture, but since I am now a free man, let me warn you that there are 299 Roman youths waiting impatiently for their chance to do what I have failed to achieve today. I was the one who had the honour to be first in line.'

On his return to Rome, Mucius received a hero's welcome. No one had expected to see him again and when he explained how he had sacrificed his arm, he was awarded the title *Scaevola*, which means 'Left-handed'. The Romans generally regarded left-handed people as sinister, hence the Latin word *sinister*, which also means 'left-handed', but Mucius received the title as an honorific.

Lars was now thoroughly perturbed. He had no desire to risk his life to save Tarquin's political skin, since he judged him to be a villainous scoundrel. Accordingly he decided to sue for peace. He knew he couldn't completely betray Tarquin's cause without losing face, however, so he

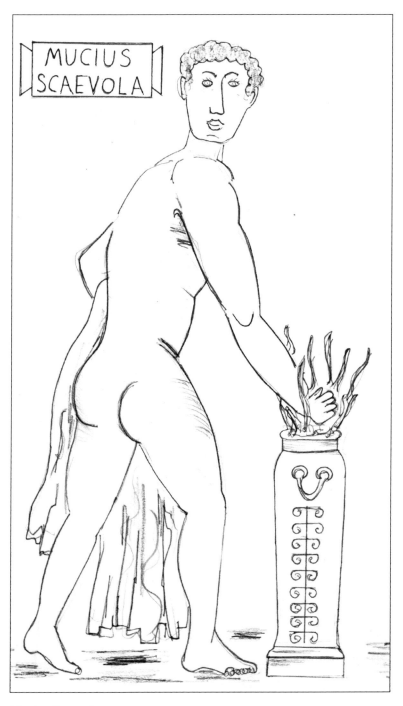

Mucius Scaevola.

offered to abandon the siege on condition that the Romans agreed to receive their king back. The Senate naturally refused as he knew they would. It was an empty, face-saving gesture. Next, he offered to withdraw if they would send hostages to him, both youths and virgins, as proof of their goodwill towards Clusium. Though mortified, the Romans had no appetite for further hostilities and reluctantly agreed.

Lars Porsena was about to learn that the patriotism of Roman girls was just as impressive as that of Roman youths. Under cover of darkness one of the hostage girls, whose name was Cloelia, succeeded in slipping through the Etruscan lines before she plunged headlong into the Tiber, along with several other girls whom she had persuaded to accompany her. Before they were halfway across, the alarm was raised and the Etruscans began hurling javelins into the water. All the girls succeeded in swimming

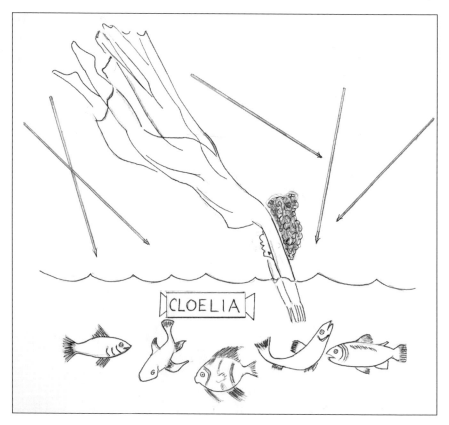

Cloelia.

safely to the other side, however, and Cloelia was congratulated for her courage and resolution in outsmarting the Etruscans.

There followed one of the most stirring actions of which we have report from antiquity. Lars, yet again, was furious. The Romans, as he saw it, had broken their agreement. He demanded that Cloelia be returned to him forthwith. He said that if they complied, he would restore her to them unharmed. It was, he said, to be a test of their adherence to international law. Amazingly the Romans agreed to his demand and handed Cloelia back. Even more astonishingly, Lars kept to his side of the bargain and returned the girl as promised.

Lars had no further interest in lending support to Tarquin. He was done. It had cost him too dear already and he feared every footfall in the night. He told him so and the king and his family departed from his territory.

Tarquin now sought assistance from the Latins, Rome's immediate neighbours. He was able to put pressure on them because he was related to them by marriage – their leader happened to be his son-in-law. A battle took place at Lake Regillus, whose exact site is unknown, in the year 499. The encounter was part of a protracted struggle between the Romans and the Latins for control of the region surrounding Rome – a struggle whose origins went back to the days of Father Aeneas. The battle resulted in a resounding victory for the Romans, thanks in large part to the intervention of Castor and Pollux, the Heavenly Twins, who, as Wikipedia points out, were conceived in consequence of 'heteropaternal superfecundation', which means they had different mothers.

The Roman commander Postumius had promised before the battle to dedicate a temple to the Heavenly Twins in the Forum, if they would lend him their support. After the victory, he was as good as his word. Three columns supporting a fragment of the entablature is all that survives of this temple, which was erected at the spot where the Heavenly Twins stopped to water their horses after the battle.

Tarquin retired to southern Italy and was never heard of again. His son Sextus, Lucretia's rapist, sought shelter in a Latin town called Gabii, ten miles east of Rome. He had previously betrayed Gabii to the Romans by pretending he had fallen out with his father and then delivering its inhabitants over to him. They hadn't forgotten his duplicity and struck him down as soon as he arrived.

The Temple of Castor and Pollux.

Chapter 14

Coriolanus Banishes Rome

Rome, not having been built in a day, was continuing to grow by leaps and bounds. It had already become one of the few places in the world where you could engage the services of stonemasons, beauticians, tanners, scribes, bricklayers, ditch diggers, mortar mixers, charcoal burners, knife grinders, flautists, harpists, lute players, lapidaries, customised glassware manufacturers, gold and silver merchants, fullers, lamp factors, woodcarvers, plasterers, potters, mould makers, cameo engravers, house painters, horse doctors, chaplet and wreath makers, customised breastplate manufacturers, makers of portable braziers, weatherproof awning vendors, importers of domesticated exotic birds, carvers of statues in the shape of satyrs and fauns, hypocaust heating system contractors, soothsayers specialising in short-term prophecies, soothsayers specialising in long-term prophecies, composers of metrical epitaphs in honour of low- and middle-ranking government officials, purveyors of unblemished sacrificial chickens (by appointment to the College of Augurs), *et al.* As the satirist Juvenal would later put it, 'Everything is available in Rome for a price.'

Yet while Rome continued to expand and attract foreigners, it still faced ongoing threats from its neighbours. It wasn't only the Etruscans and the Latins who gave Rome grief. So, too, did the Aequians, the Volscians, the Samnites, and others too numerous to mention. All these peoples would have liked nothing better than to wipe the upstart city from the face of the earth.

It was now, too, that a deep division, long simmering beneath the surface, arose between the Senate and the commons, otherwise called the plebs. The two were known collectively by the acronym SPQR, which stand for *Senatus PopulusQue Romanus,* meaning 'The Senate and the Roman People'. The phrase expresses the indissoluble union between the two arms of the Republic. It was not always the case that this union was indissoluble, however. Indeed on several occasions in Rome's early history the plebs was minded to secede, abandon Rome, and constitute itself into a separate state.

And that is exactly what happened about a generation or so after the establishment of the Republic. A bunch of disgruntled commoners set up camp on the Aventine Hill. Panic reigned among the aristocrats. There were fears of a general uprising, as well as fears of a foreign invasion by one of Rome's many enemies, ready to take advantage of the crisis. Fortunately, nothing came of it, largely due to the intervention of a senator called Agrippa Menenius Lenatus, who came up with a rather novel analogy to justify aristocratic privilege.

'It was once the case', Menenius told the rebels, 'that the various parts of the body began to resent the fact that they toiled endlessly just to put food into the belly, whereas the belly just sat on its backside, so to speak, and did nothing. Accordingly, they decided they would no longer serve their master but instead serve themselves. That, they surmised, would teach the belly a lesson. Well, it wasn't long before the other parts of the body began to waste away. They realised just in time that the belly is by no means otiose. With the food it receives and digests, it nourishes these other parts, which, being fortified, promote the welfare and safety of the whole. The belly therefore deserves favourable treatment, as do we, the aristocrats, who are constantly labouring to advance *your* welfare and safety.'

Not all those in attendance understood the point of the analogy but a sufficient number did, and the disaster of civil strife was averted. To appease the populace, the Senate appointed representatives called tribunes of the people, whose task it was to protect the populace against abuses by the consuls and others. Even so, resentment on both sides continued to fester in the body politic.

It is at this point in history that one of Rome's most controversial, if fictional, heroes steps onto the stage, an aristocrat by the name of Gaius Marcius. While Rome was still recovering from its recent unrest, a people called the Volscians, who inhabited a region to the south of Rome, had launched a surprise attack from Corioli, their leading city. They might well have succeeded in breaching Rome's defences, were it not for the vigilance of Gaius Marcius.

Marcius wasn't content just to save Rome, however. Having forced the Volscians back to Corioli, he burst into the city through a gate that had been opened to receive the survivors. Once inside, he seized a firebrand

and hurled it onto a thatched roof. His comrades did likewise and before long the whole city was in flames. In this way Corioli fell to the Romans. On his return Marcius was hailed as Rome's saviour and in recognition of his services granted the honorific title 'Coriolanus'.

Rome was still in a bad way, however. Because of the social divisions, work in the fields had been suspended. Many of the populace, including slaves, of whom there was already a large number, were facing starvation. Accordingly, the consuls sent agents abroad to purchase as much grain as they could.

Most senators thought that the only way to heal the deep divisions and protect the plebs was by drastically reducing the price of corn. However, this policy wasn't without its critics. Its foremost opponent was the newly named Coriolanus, the sworn foe of the rights of ordinary people, which he saw as inimical to the interests of the aristocracy. Accordingly, when a debate took place in the Senate about subsidising the price of grain, he made his feelings known in no uncertain terms.

'Why in the name of Castor and Pollux should we give cut-price grain to the indolent mob?' he thundered. 'What have the plebs ever done for Rome? They're merely an idle bunch of wastrels, ne'er-do-wells leeching off those of us who put our lives at risk for the common good. Idle mouths, that's what they are. They're a perpetual drain on our resources. Toss them out of Rome, I say. Let them steal to stay alive. That's all they're good at – stealing. If they want cheap grain, they must offer us something in turn. Let them give up the tribunate. Tribunes are a canker at the heart of the Republic.'

Many senators were in fervent agreement about the danger posed to their privileges by the tribunate, but none dared openly to support him. They all feared for their lives. The tension between the ruling body and the plebs was reaching boiling point. Very likely Coriolanus would have been assaulted when leaving the Senate after giving such an inflammatory speech, were it not – paradoxically – for the intervention of the tribunes, who now stepped forward, charged him with conspiring to undermine the interests and safety of the plebs, and held the angry mob at bay.

Coriolanus looked at the tribunes scornfully. 'After all that I've done for Rome, this is all the thanks I get? Well, you'll damn well have to do without my services in the future. I've had it with Rome. It's populated with snivelling malcontents who do nothing but bitch and moan.'

'OK, that's it', the leading tribune said without further ado. 'I'll have you banished for disrespecting the plebs.'

'Banished, did you say?' repeated Coriolanus with a snarl of contempt. 'On the contrary, I banish Rome.'

So saying, Coriolanus stormed off. He bade farewell to his family – his wife, mother and two small sons – and departed that same day. The tribunes through their Council condemned him to death *in absentia*.

Not a man to indulge in half measures, Coriolanus headed straight to the Volscians. He was determined to wreak vengeance on Rome. He slipped through the enemy lines disguised as a beggar and, after making inquiries of one of the locals, headed towards the house of Aufidius, the Volscian commander. Arriving, he banged loudly on the door.

Coriolanus contemplates his banishment.

'Tell your master that Gaius Marcius, the man who destroyed Corioli, is waiting attendance on him', he said to the pair of eyes that appeared when a latch was drawn back.

The doorkeeper's jaw dropped as he stared long and hard at the man standing before him.

'Well, did you hear me?' Coriolanus menaced.

'Yes, of course, yes', the slave stammered. 'Please wait here.' Then he shuffled off down the vestibule, the soles of his feet flapping on the tiled floor.

Seconds later he returned. 'My master will see you', he said.

Inside the atrium, Coriolanus observed that Aufidius was in session with his senior officers. He stood to military attention and struck his breast.

'Most noble Attius Tullius Aufidius, my name is Gaius Marcius. I'm the man who destroyed Corioli. I'm here to place myself at your mercy. I'm not here to sue for my life. You can kill me for all I care. I know I deserve it for the grief I have caused your people. But if you choose to spare me, I make a solemn promise that I will be your most fervent ally, just as I was once your most fervent enemy. The Romans have incurred my undying hate for making light of the wounds that I received in defending them. Let us join hands and wreak havoc on Rome and all who inhabit it.'

'Well, this is an unexpected turn of events', Aufidius replied mildly, scratching his stubbly chin and looking the stranger up and down. 'You're the last person I was ever expecting to meet face to face. Tell me in more detail why you have decided to betray your city and what makes you think I should trust you.'

Coriolanus proceeded to explain how it had come about that he felt so much venom towards his compatriots. When he came to the end of his story, Aufidius, who had listened attentively throughout, said, 'Very well, I'll place some of my men under your command. I'll soon see if your hatred towards Rome is genuine. If it isn't, if this is some kind of trick, be assured you will die an agonising death.'

Over the next few months, the Volscians, under the joint leadership of Coriolanus and Aufidius, won back many of the towns that the Romans had taken. Eventually they were ready for a direct assault on Rome itself. They had pitched their camp a short distance from the city.

Even now, with the prospect of Rome being utterly destroyed, Coriolanus' fury towards his countrymen remained unabated. The Senate dispatched ambassadors to propose peace terms but to no avail. The man was inflexible.

It was at this point that a group of women decided as a last resort to entreat Volumnia and Veturia, Coriolanus' wife and mother, to appeal to him. When they arrived at their house, they saw that its walls had been smeared with pitch and daubed with obscene graffiti. The door hung crookedly, suggesting that someone had tried to tear it from its hinges.

Volumnia and Veturia were squatting on the floor of the atrium. They were playing with Coriolanus' young sons. Both looked startled when the women were shown in. It was clear that their nerves were in shreds.

'There's nothing to be afraid of', the oldest of the women said. 'We're merely here to ask for your help. Marcius is about to attack Rome. He may do so at any moment. If he does, and the Volscians capture our city, they will show us – and you – no mercy. Naked babies will be spitted upon pikes. Children and the elderly will be put to the sword. Women will be raped. He's refused all offers from the Senate to make amends for the indignity he has suffered. Our only hope – Rome's only hope – is that he will listen to an appeal from his mother and wife. Men have tried in vain to win him over. Perhaps women will succeed where they couldn't.'

It didn't take long to persuade Volumnia and Veturia to agree. Rome was on the ropes owing to Coriolanus' treasonable behaviour and here was an opportunity to rid themselves of their awful burden of guilt. They rose, hugged their visitors, told the two little boys to fetch their cloaks, and left immediately. It took them all day to reach the Volscian camp, since Veturia could walk only with difficulty. Once they gained the surrounding palisade, they were permitted to pass through the lines, such was their pitiable condition.

When a Volscian soldier informed Coriolanus that some Romans were seeking an audience with him, he refused to have anything to do with them.

'Haven't these accursed people got the point yet?' he demanded, turning away scornfully. 'Nothing will move me at this point. Nothing will lessen my hatred. Not appeals from senators, not appeals from priests, not appeals from commoners.'

'I don't think this is an official delegation, Gaius Marcius', the soldier said. 'They look as if they've come on their own initiative. Two women and two young boys. Could they be relatives by any chance?'

Coriolanus spun around. 'Ye gods, Veturia and Volumnia and my sons are here? They must be desperate. I'll have to acknowledge them. But first I must ask permission from Aufidius. I don't want him to think I would betray our solemn agreement. Tell them to wait outside my tent. I'll be back.'

He immediately set off to find Aufidius. He was in his tent, having his hair plaited by a comely slave boy.

'Forgive this intrusion, Attius. My wife and mother wish to see me. Will you permit that? I assure you that Rome is as hateful to me now as it was when I first offered you my services. I merely wish to explain my decision to them. I solemnly swear I will never set eyes on them again.'

In recent days Aufidius had begun to harbour a grudge against Coriolanus, whose military talents far outstripped his. The Roman was even beginning to outdo him in the popularity stakes among the Volscian army. So, he told Coriolanus that he was free to do as he chose, privately hoping that this encounter would provide him with an excuse to rid himself of a dangerous rival. Now that the Volscians were poised to attack Rome, moreover, he no longer felt in need of his assistance.

Coriolanus returned to his tent, where his family was now waiting. For a few moments he stood stock still, uncertain what to say to any of them. Then he took a hesitant step towards his mother and tried to embrace her, but she pushed him roughly aside.

'I'm not here today as your mother', Veturia said sternly. 'I'm here as *every* Roman mother. It's been my lot in life to see my son first as a saviour, then as an outcast, and now as a traitor. I understand why you feel hatred towards the Senate and the common people. They have treated you abominably. I'm not here to suggest you should change your opinion of them. But don't you have any concern for your family or for the land that nurtured you or for the gods in whose name you fought so valiantly? Look at your sons here – are you about to slay them? Look at your wife – are you about to hand her over to the lust of the Volscians? Look at your mother – are you about to condemn her to the most sorrowful ending to life that a mother could imagine? Make no mistake, Gaius, these will be the consequences of your pride, no matter how justified your anger.'

When Veturia finished speaking, his sons, unprompted, ran forward and threw themselves at their father's feet. Coriolanus could bear it no longer. Tears began to roll down his cheeks. He beckoned his wife and mother, and all embraced.

THE APPEAL TO CORIOLANUS

Coriolanus' family make their appeal (after Gavin Hamilton).

'You have prevailed', he said, drying his tears. 'I cannot be part of an action that would put you at risk. I will no longer lead my Volscian contingent against Rome. I still think that Rome was wrong to yield to the plebs and that the plebs are deserving of contempt. But that is beside the point. You can tell the Senate that I am no longer Rome's enemy. I will never be her friend, mind you. But I have ceased to be her enemy.'

Coriolanus departed that same day. Aufidius was not displeased. Even so, his assault on Rome stalled. He later joined arms with the Aequians, a neighbouring people who lived to the east of Rome, but in the ensuing encounter his forces were defeated.

We don't know what happened to Coriolanus after this. One account is that Aufidius had him assassinated. Another is that he lived out his days in bitterness and despondency. Either way, true to his word, he never set foot in Rome again.

Chapter 15

Cincinnatus, Dictator for Fifteen Days

Rome's troubles with her neighbours rumbled on, as did the bitterness between the plebs and the aristocracy. The people weren't content merely to have tribunes to safeguard their interests. What they now wanted was a written lawcode. Only if they had a written lawcode, they argued, would they be proof against summary justice. As things stood, a commoner could be hauled before a judge for some petty crime, which, at the whim of that judge, turned out to be punishable by death. You'd think that the demand for a written lawcode would have been regarded as just, but many aristocrats, jealous of their right to mete out summary justice, saw this as the thin end of the wedge.

'Give a commoner an inch and he'll take a mile', they argued. 'Once we no longer have the right to decide what is and isn't a criminal action or to inflict whatever punishment we see fit, there'll be no stopping the wretches. Besides, the demand for a written lawcode is an insult to our innate sense of justice, which, as we all know, gets passed down to us through our lineage.'

One young aristocrat called Caeso Quinctius Cincinnatus was particularly violent in his opposition to a written lawcode. He became the ringleader of a right-wing band of thugs, who went around roughing up anyone who demonstrated support for the plebs. Caeso was a nasty piece of work. One day he broke into the house of a political opponent and beat the man savagely to death. His victim had been sick at the time, which made the crime all the more despicable. The victim's brother appealed to the tribunes and an order was issued for Caeso's arrest. Before he could be apprehended, however, he fled to the Etruscans. He was condemned to death *in absentia*.

Judgement now fell upon Caeso's father, Lucius Quinctius Cincinnatus, a former consul and highly respected senator. Cincinnatus, though equally opposed to the plebs gaining more power, had never broken the law. However, the fact that he was held in high regard could not shield him from the consequences of his son's recklessness. He was ordered to pay a huge fine and in consequence forced to sell off his property in Rome. He also had to resign from the Senate, since only wealthy landowners could hold senatorial rank.

Cincinnatus was not, however, downcast. On the contrary, he saw positive advantages in the humble life. He bought a small farm, just three acres in extent, to which he retired with his devoted wife of forty years, Racilia.

Fate had not yet done with Cincinnatus, however. Two years later the Aequians began making incursions into Roman territory. The two peoples had locked horns repeatedly in the past, most recently during the time of Coriolanus. Such was the threat they now posed that the Senate dispatched both consular armies to quell them. Consuls were military leaders and each commanded his own army.

News then reached the city that the Aequians had destroyed one of the armies, along with its consul, and that the other, under a certain Minucius, was completely encircled. Panic gripped the Senate. It resolved that the only course of action was to appoint a dictator. But who? Eventually, it decided that the only man who could see them through a crisis of this magnitude was Cincinnatus. Accordingly it straightway sent a deputation to his farm to offer him the post.

The dictatorship was an official position within the structure of the Republic. It was granted to an individual for a limited period of time – six months at most – and for the accomplishment of a specific goal. The goal in this case was to defeat the Aequians.

When a deputation of senators arrived at Cincinnatus' farm to make him the offer, it was raining. They found the elderly Cincinnatus guiding his plough behind a team of oxen. The senators traipsed across a mud-soaked field, avoiding fetid puddles and clods of dung. The man was dressed in a threadbare tunic that barely covered his knees. His lower legs were encrusted with mud. Sweat was pouring down his face. He looked anything but a likely candidate for the dictatorship.

'Hello, illustrious gentlemen, this is a surprise', he said, looking up from his plough and shielding his eyes from the glare of the sun with his grimy hand. 'What's going on? Is everything all right?'

'You haven't heard?' the most senior member of the deputation demanded. 'We're about to be overrun by the Aequians.'

'The Aequians? Are they on the rampage again? Thanks for the warning. It's very kind of you to come all this way to tell me.'

'That's not why we came, Lucius, and this isn't just normal rampaging stuff. It's far more serious than that. But before we tell you why we're here, I wonder if you would mind putting on a toga. We're here on official business, and, well, no disrespect but it isn't appropriate that we conduct it with you dressed in your working clothes.'

Cincinnatus stared hard at the man. 'You want me to put on a toga? Are you serious? I haven't worn one in years.' When they made no reply, he shrugged, cupped his hands around his mouth, and bellowed in the direction of his hovel, 'Racilia, would you mind fetching me my toga? If my memory serves me, I think you'll find it in that small chest I keep in the outhouse. It'll be buried beneath my workaday togs. It's probably a bit dusty, not to say moth-eaten. You'd better shake it out in the yard.'

Then turning to the senators, he said, 'If you don't mind, I'll take a quick bathe.'

Cincinnatus handed the plough to a slave and trudged off. He was something of a handyman and had constructed an outdoor shower by storing water in a terracotta basin on the roof of his outhouse. When he turned the tap on, the water sluiced down a lead pipe attached to the side of the building.

It is not clear whether Cincinnatus took a wash in deference to the toga he was about to don or whether he did so to incommode his visitors. The fact of the matter is that he kept them standing in a mud-soaked field in a drizzle for a full hour.

'Well now, what is this official business that brought you all this distance?' he inquired, as he ambled back. He was clutching the hem of his toga around his stomach to avoid getting it soiled in the mud.

'The fact of the matter is, Lucius', the leading delegate began, 'we – I mean Rome - is in a complete mess. We, Rome that is, don't have anyone whom we trust to see us through this crisis except, well, except you. We were wondering – we were hoping – that you might agree to step into the breach. We realise that – well, not to put too fine a point upon it – you may feel some resentment for losing all your money, but the law is the law and the current crisis is of such magnitude that we are here to appeal to your better nature in the expectation that both sides – you and us, I mean – can leave partisanship behind.'

'Exactly what breach are you hoping I might step into, illustrious gentlemen?' Cincinnatus demanded, bending over to scrape mud off the blade of his plough with a rusty nail.

'Well, we – that is the Senate – would like to appoint you dictator so that you can lead our troops against the Aequians.'

Cincinnatus straightened his back and examined the face of each delegate in turn.

'Is this some sort of a joke, gentlemen? I'm turning sixty next month. Surely there's somebody more suitable. I can barely mount a horse these days. Besides, who's going to mind my farm in my absence?'

'You're our best hope, Lucius', pleaded the leading delegate. 'All the senators are at each other's throats. You know what they're like in a crisis. They can't agree about anything. The only thing they *can* agree about is that you're the best – actually the *only* man for the job. If you don't come to our aid, the Aequians will destroy us. We're half-destroyed already. And by the way, if you still bear a grudge for being deprived of your wealth, this would be a great opportunity to get even. You'll have absolute power to do whatever you like.'

'Absolute power doesn't interest me in the least', Cincinnatus replied with a dismissive wave of his swarthy hand.

'Even so –'

'Even so, I reluctantly agree.'

At this the delegates heaved a collective sigh of relief. They stepped forward all eager to take his hand, but he backed away from them. Then he turned to his wife, who had come over to see what was going on. 'I'm heading to Rome, Racilia. I've got a job to do. I'll be back in a few days.'

'Don't count on it, Lucius', one of the delegates said warily.

'You can count on it, Racilia', Cincinnatus replied sternly. 'I'll be back in a few days.'

Cincinnatus headed to Rome that night, accompanied by the delegation. The next morning he was sworn in as Rome's fifth dictator.

'OK', he said to the gathering, once the swearing-in ceremony was over. 'Here are my orders. I'm placing Rome on a war footing. That means all shops are to close effective nightfall and all public business is suspended till further notice. Every man between the age of eighteen and fifty-five is to turn up at the Campus Martius at dawn tomorrow with his military equipment. Only those at death's door or with a medical note are excused. You're going to need rations for five days – onions, radishes, a loaf of bread, cheese if you have it, sour wine, that sort of thing. If you're fifty-six or over, you're to help the younger men get their stuff ready. You can cook bread or something. I don't care what.

Just do something useful. We all need to muck in. This is a national emergency. Every conscript has to bring twelve stakes with him as well. It doesn't matter how you get hold of the stakes. You can steal them from your neighbour for all I care. Oh, and you're all going to need a shovel. There's going to be some digging. Any questions? Good. Get to it. We're going to teach those damned Aequians a lesson they won't forget.'

A loud cheer went up. Suddenly everyone felt a lot better. The populace dispersed and prepared for the upcoming campaign. All day the city was seething with activity. At dawn the next day the Campus Martius was packed with troops.

'OK, men', Cincinnatus said, taking his stand on a tribunal. 'Just remember that the future of Rome lies in your hands. You're her last best hope. One consular army has been wiped out. Another is surrounded and faces imminent destruction. Now here's the plan. I want you all to line up behind the standard bearer over there. We're going to take the Aequians by surprise, so once we get within a mile of their camp, you're to proceed in absolute silence. If anybody so much as coughs, I'll have him crucified – literally. Then, once we're within shouting distance of the Aequians, I'll give the signal for you to tiptoe around their camp in a circle. As soon as you're in place, I'll give another signal and when you hear that one, you're to raise the war cry. Make it as blood-curdling and nerve-tingling as you can. This will not only rattle the Aequians but also indicate to Consul Minucius that help has arrived. He'll then launch an attack against the Aequians so that they face inward in his direction. As soon as the fighting begins, start furiously digging a ditch around the Aequian camp so that you hem them in. When that's done, fix your stakes in the earth that you've thrown up behind the ditch. In other words, you're going to construct what is called in military jargon a circumvallation. Once it's completed, I'll give you the order to attack and the Aequians will have to face opposition on two fronts at once. OK then, off we go. Look sharpish, everyone. *Dex, sin, dex sin, dex, sin.*'

Everything went according to clockwork. Though many of his troops hadn't seen military service before, all had complete confidence in Cincinnatus. They arrived at the enemy camp without being noticed, surrounded it and took the Aequians completely off guard. Minucius' army understood that help had arrived and immediately launched an attack from the inside. Soon the Aequians found themselves surrounded and were fighting on two fronts at once. They were quickly forced to sue for peace.

Cincinnatus dreams of being back on his farm.

To deter the Aequians from the thought of ever taking up arms against the Romans again, Cincinnatus ordered two spears to be stuck in the ground and a horizontal spear to be mounted on top. The Aequians were then lined up and each man was compelled to bow his head under a yoke of spears, much to the derision of the Romans. It was similar to the punishment that had been meted out to Publius Horatius centuries ago.

'That'll teach you not to mess with Romans in the future', Cincinnatus said scornfully to the Aequian commander, when the last of his men had passed under the yoke. Then he turned to Consul Minucius. 'Tell your men to gather all the property in the Aequian camp and make a big pile

A Roman trophy.

of it. I'm going to distribute it among the men I brought to relieve you. You and your lot aren't going to get a damn thing. I'm also formally stripping you of the title of consul. You're a disgrace to the Roman name. If we hadn't arrived when we did, your army would have been wiped out, like that of your consular colleague. Count yourself lucky that I didn't force *you* to go under the yoke.'

Cincinnatus was granted a triumph – a uniquely Roman way of celebrating a military victory. The day before it took place his army mustered outside the city on the Campus Martius. The triumphal procession entered on the west side of the city and made its way to the Forum along the Sacred Way.

At its head was the Aequian commander, led in shackles. Then came carts laden with spoils. Magistrates and other worthies walked beside the carts. Next came the star of the show, the *triumphator* himself, riding in a chariot in full armour, cheeks reddened. Standing beside him was a slave, who kept whispering in his ear, 'Remember you're mortal'. This was to prevent his ego from getting the better of him, which, if it had done so, would have aroused the envy of the gods. Cincinnatus' soldiers followed behind, dressed in togas to indicate that they posed no threat to

A Roman triumph.

the civil order. A massive sacrifice to Jupiter was performed and after the god had received his portion, the rest of the meat was distributed to the populace. It was, one might say, an orgy of self-congratulation.

Cincinnatus had performed the task for which he had been appointed with distinction. He could have held onto the dictatorship longer by claiming he had to 'tidy up loose ends', had he not been a man of exemplary integrity. Instead he resigned immediately. He was justifiably regarded as one of Rome's greatest heroes, not only because of his military accomplishment but also because of his distaste for untrammelled power.

'Hello, dear', he called out to Racilia, when he opened the door of his farmhouse fifteen days later. 'I'm home.'

Chapter 16

An Honour Killing

It's one of the striking features of the Republic that in the first centuries of its existence political turmoil was the order of the day. Things reached such a pitch two years after Cincinnatus' victory over the Aequians that the Senate took the unprecedented step of suspending the constitution. In place of magistrates, it appointed a Decemvirate or Board of Ten.

The chief reason for the turmoil was the fact that the legal system was in a complete mess. There were still no written laws, which meant that everybody was still arguing about what was and wasn't a crime and what punishment should be meted out.

In the first year that the Board of Ten took charge things went fairly smoothly. Each day a different *decemvir* was in charge, so no individual was able to amass power. Together the Ten drafted written laws, which they inscribed on bronze tablets. They administered justice fairly.

At the end of the year a certain Appius Claudius Crassus Sabinus Regillensis, the most high-handed of the Ten, made it known that he intended to stand for election again. A rigged election was held, and Appius was re-appointed. All the other nine *decemvirs* were his close allies.

It was now that things took a very ominous turn. Previously only the *decemvir* in charge that day had been permitted to be accompanied by lictors, the officials who bore the *fasces*, the bundles of rods and axes I mentioned earlier. Now, however, every *decemvir* appeared in public accompanied by his own set of lictors – twelve apiece. The populace saw this as a sign of their extra-judicial authority, since every *decemvir* was now free to punish whomever he liked without reference to the law, written or otherwise. And when the *decemvirs* appeared in public together, the sight of 120 lictors bearing *fasces* struck fear and loathing into the populace. It was as if the Ten had a private army at their disposal.

There now began a veritable reign of terror, the like of which Rome had never seen before. It was the plebs who suffered most, being subject to summary beatings and execution. The right of appeal was abolished and adherence to due process flew out of the window. Free speech was curtailed and every officer in the state was appointed by the Board of Ten. It had been bad enough when Rome was ruled by one tyrant, people started saying. Now they were ruled by ten.

Like many before and after him, Appius abused his power to satisfy his lust. He set his eye on a beautiful plebeian girl in her late teens called Verginia, who was the daughter of a highly decorated centurion. When Verginius, the father, was posted outside Rome, Appius determined to take advantage of his absence to have his way with his daughter.

At first Appius tried to seduce Verginia with presents and favours. This had always worked for him in the past but the girl would have none of it. She was betrothed to a young man called Lucius Icilius and had no intention of betraying her beloved. Once Appius realised that his blandishments were getting him nowhere, he decided to resort to cunning. He persuaded one of his clients – a client in Roman terms is someone who owes you a favour – to claim that Verginia was a fugitive slave.

The client, whose name was Marcus Claudius, bided his time. Then, observing her one morning strolling through the Forum accompanied by her nurse, he grabbed her arm and shouted, 'You thought you could run off, did you? I know your sort all too well. I'll teach you a lesson. You come home with me now.'

Then, turning to address the small crowd of bystanders which had gathered around him, he explained, 'This here girl is my slave. She ran off last month. I've been looking for her everywhere. What effrontery to be walking through the Forum!'

Verginia was dumbstruck. 'You must be mistaking me for someone else, sir', she said, trying unsuccessfully to loosen his grip on her arm. 'I've never seen you in my life before. I'm not a slave. I'm the daughter of a centurion.'

'The daughter of a centurion? That's a good one', Marcus said, snorting derisively. Then, turning again to the crowd, he said, 'Slaves these days. I tell you. They think they can get away with anything. They don't have any respect for their masters. They're always scheming and stealing and talking back. I don't know what Rome is coming to. I'm too lenient, that's my problem. This isn't the first time she's done this. I should have had her beaten when she ran away before. Now she's paying me back by running off again. All right. If the girl won't come

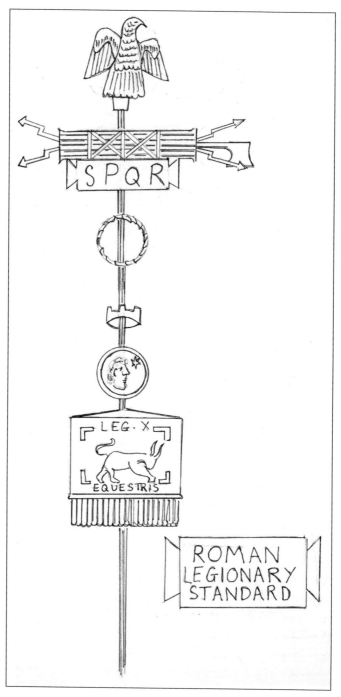

A Roman legionary standard.

home with me, I'll bring her to court. I want what's mine. The judge will determine whether I get it.'

There was nothing Verginia could do. In fact there was nothing that any young girl born into poverty could have done in such a situation. It was a fact that many attractive young girls of plebeian background ended up in slavery in this way. In the absence of birth certificates, paternity, particularly a girl's paternity, was often impossible to prove. Sex trafficking is as old as the hills.

Verginia had no option but to accompany her accuser to a judge. All she could think was that the man was making a genuine mistake. She told her nurse to contact her friends, who scraped together some money to pay for a lawyer. The lawyer argued that her trial should be postponed until the man she swore was her father could be present, whereupon the judge referred the decision to Appius, as had been planned all along.

Appius ordered Verginius to be recalled to Rome. Since Verginia was deemed to be a flight risk, however, he ordered that she be bound over to the plaintiff, pending the arrival of Verginius. All he wanted was to take Verginia's virginity.

Things did not quite go according to Appius' plan, however. Just after he had banged his gavel, or the ancient Roman equivalent thereof, Icilius, Verginia's fiancé, burst into the courtroom. He had heard what had happened and had run immediately to the courthouse. The lictors did their best to restrain him but could not silence him.

'I know your game!' Icilius shouted. 'I'm not going to permit my beloved Verginia to become the victim of hot and forcing violation. In the name of all the gods, in the name of all that's holy, in the name of the chaste goddess Diana, I appeal to the people of Rome to protect my bride. I'll tell Verginius what you're up to and he'll raise an army to come after you, you mark my words! You think that every Roman girl is here to serve your lust. Well think again!'

Realising that the crowd's sympathies lay with Icilius and that his reputation was at stake, Appius made a show of liberality.

'Come, come, young man', he said, smiling broadly. 'There's no need to get all worked up. I don't know what you take me for, but I would never take advantage of an innocent girl. I have always lived my life according to the highest standards of rectitude. However, I do not wish the least suspicion to attach to my office. I therefore agree to release the defendant on bail until tomorrow, by which time I expect the man she alleges to be her father be present in my court. It's entirely possible that the centurion has been duped as well. Perhaps the girl turned up on his doorstep one day, claiming to be his long-lost daughter. Who knows? Anyway, if he doesn't make a court appearance, I will take that as an indication that he has no connection with the defendant and give judgement in favour of the plaintiff.'

Verginia's friends again pooled their resources so that she could post bail. Icilius didn't lose a second. He borrowed a horse and galloped to the camp where Verginius was stationed and explained what had happened with a letter from the court authorising his release. Meanwhile, Appius sent a courier to Verginius' commanding officer declaring the court order null and void and demanding that he keep the centurion at his post until further notice. By the time his courier arrived, however, Icilius and Verginius were on their way to Rome.

Verginius, accompanied by his daughter and her nurse, entered the court before cockcrow the next morning. News of their case had spread throughout the city and a huge crowd of well-wishers had gathered to greet them. Many people saw it as a test of the power of the Board of Ten to flout justice. Appius did his best to conceal his rage at the appearance of the centurion but was inwardly fuming.

When Verginius took the stand to bear witness, everyone fell silent. 'Please know how grateful I am to all of you who have turned up today to give me and my daughter your support', he began, speaking loudly so that his voice would carry outside the courtroom. 'I am a patriot through and through, a loyal servant of the Republic, an army man with more than twenty years of service under his belt and with the scars to prove it, one who puts his life in harm's way routinely in the service of the fatherland. But I am not here today to defend Rome against its enemies. I am here to defend my daughter and myself. It is unthinkable that my paternity should be challenged. I swear solemnly in the name of all the immortal gods that I am indeed Verginia's father. If the verdict goes against me, no daughter, no wife, no mother will be safe.'

The trial turned out to be a complete travesty of justice. Marcus Claudius, the plaintiff, couldn't produce a single witness to back up his assertion that Verginia had once been his slave. Despite this fact, Appius found in Marcus' favour, claiming that Verginius had failed to prove he was the girl's father. His judgement given, he ordered Verginia to be arrested, whereupon two of his lictors stepped forward, seized the girl by both arms, and thrust her into Marcus' hands.

The crowd reacted to the seizure of the girl with outrage, and Appius became greatly alarmed.

'Lictors, see that the people disperse at once!' he shouted. 'The Republic is in danger. I've reason to believe that among Verginius' supporters there is a revolutionary faction intent on unseating the Board of Ten. They've been using this case to defame me. Judging by Verginius' words, it's pretty clear that the army is infected with the same virus. This is all part of a deep plot. Immediate action is called for to safeguard Rome's survival. We must root out the traitors!'

The lictors raised their rods and began striking indiscriminately at all who stood in their path. Soon they had cleared an empty space around Verginius.

'Most honoured *decemvir*, forgive me for my rashness', the centurion declared, falling on one knee and humbly bowing his head. 'The almighty gods know that I never intended to insult either you or the dignity of your office. I am certainly not part of any conspiracy. My poor petition is that that you allow me a brief space to question the woman who claims to be her nurse. I have served in so many wars that I have had little opportunity to be at home and know my daughter – if she is indeed my daughter – even slightly. If the nurse cannot provide me with incontrovertible proof that I am her father, I will accept your judgement and acknowledge that I have been cruelly deceived. Please grant a loyal Roman this small favour. The plot uncovered, I will return this miscreant to the court.'

Appius was completely taken in by this apparent show of remorse and willingness to submit to his authority. Things had turned out far better than he could have hoped for. With an extravagant display of magnanimity, he agreed to grant Verginius' request. Verginius thanked him effusively and then, accompanied by his daughter and her nurse, left the court and made his way to the shops where meat was sold, just a short distance from the Forum.

There he grabbed a butcher's knife from one of the vendors, dragged Verginia to the nearby shrine of Venus Cloacina, that's to say, Venus of the Sewer, and plunged it deep into her heart. The girl fell to the ground and bled out within minutes, producing a thin trickle of blood that stained the flagstones as it flowed down a slight incline.

Verginius stands over the body of his murdered daughter.

'My daughter will never be a slave to a tyrant's lust!' Verginius exclaimed triumphantly.

When Appius heard what had happened, he ordered his lictors to seize the centurion. It was too late. Verginius had made a dash to one of the city gates where his horse was tethered. Within minutes, he was galloping back to his army.

He rode into camp covered in blood and still clutching the bloody knife. He dismounted from his horse and told his commanding officer what had happened.

'I have sacrificed my daughter for the sake of all women', he declared. 'I know it was a terrible thing to do, but I had to take a stand. A woman's honour is more precious than life itself. If I'd let that foul creature rape her, no woman would have been safe from his lust.'

An enormous wave of sympathy arose for Verginius, both among the populace and among the military. The case had inflamed the sentiments of those already hostile to the Ten and a general outcry against their rule arose. Protests were staged throughout the land. The Senate hastily convened and the Ten agreed to resign. Appius Claudius was charged with abusing his power but hanged himself in prison before being brought to trial. A crisis had been averted and the tribunate, which the Ten had rescinded, was re-instated.

So, the plight of the plebs improved but it would be a century and a half before the *lex Hortensia*, proposed by the dictator Quintus Hortensius in 287 BCE, gave plebeian citizen assemblies the right to pass laws that were binding on the whole community.

Chapter 17

A Schoolteacher's Humiliation

Between sedition at home and wars abroad, Rome continued to be subject to upheavals on many fronts. The Etruscans to the north were down but not out. Veii, the richest city among the Etruscan League, finally fell after a long siege that had been conducted by a general called Marcus Furius Camillus. Camillus had promised to dedicate one-tenth of the spoils to Apollo if the god would assist him in achieving victory. Eventually he took the city by digging a tunnel under the city walls which connected with the sewage system. He ordered all its men to be slaughtered and the women and children to be enslaved as per normal after a siege.

It remained only to convey the Etruscan goddess Uni, Roman equivalent 'Juno', to Rome so that she wouldn't feel left out. A group of youths was appointed but before undertaking this solemn task, they took a bath and then dressed in white robes. However, just as they were about to raise her from her pedestal, they all became alarmed, fearful that the goddess would be offended.

At that precise moment, however, quite providentially, so to speak, one of the youths said, 'Hey, Juno, would you like to go to Rome?' The others cringed when they heard this, fearing they would be struck down by the informality of his address. Instead, to their utter amazement the statue nodded – they all swore on oath that this is what happened. Accordingly they tipped her over and conveyed her to the carriage that was waiting to transport her to Rome. The statue weighed next-to-nothing. It was as if the goddess was coming unaided.

Camillus was awarded a triumph, which he celebrated with unprecedented pomp and ceremony. Not for the last time in his highly distinguished career, however, he caused offence by riding in a chariot drawn by four white horses, a form of conveyance reserved exclusively for the gods. He had also broken his promise to Apollo. Rome's religious establishment was up in arms.

'Apollo is furious', the Chief Pontiff, a timorous individual with a portly belly whose eyes discharged a prodigious amount of gum,

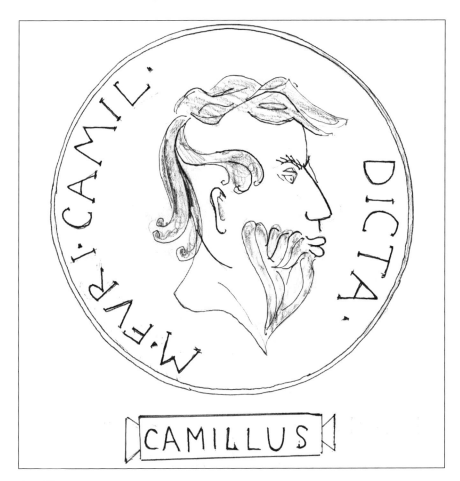

Camillus.

declared. 'You need to give him what you owe him straightaway. There's no knowing what he might do otherwise.'

'That's going to be rather difficult', Camillus pronounced in his characteristically nonchalant manner, seizing a black fly which he had observed out of the corner of his eye before hurling it to the ground and crushing it under his military boot.

The Chief Pontiff nearly jumped out of his pallid skin, unaccustomed to being challenged in this way. 'Why is it difficult?' he demanded, rubbing both eyes.

'Because I've already distributed the spoils among my soldiers. The only way I could get them to climb into the sewers was by promising them they could loot the city afterwards.'

'Then kindly ask them to return the spoils immediately.'

Fearful though the Chief Pontiff was of Camillus, it turned out that he was more fearful of Apollo.

Easier said than done. Many of the soldiers had spent their spoils already, so Camillus could recover only a small portion of what was owed. There was only one thing to do. The Senate ordered an immediate whip-round. Every Roman was required to contribute to the common fund. The most generous were the women, who donated their gold jewellery – necklaces, earrings, armbands, rings, pendants, tiaras, torques, etc. All of it was melted down and fashioned into a giant bowl, which the priest of Apollo dedicated in his temple in the Campus Martius. It was thus that the god was appeased.

Another problem arose immediately afterwards. Rome was bursting at the seams and a large percentage of the populace wanted to emigrate to Veii, which now lay abandoned. Camillus, however, was violently opposed to such a move, which he saw as spelling the end of Rome's dominance.

It was greatly to his advantage that the Etruscan war wasn't yet over, since this meant that he could persuade the populace to shelve the issue until such time as the enemy no longer posed any threat. There was one Etruscan city that was still holding out, namely Falerii, which lies thirty miles north-east of Rome. Camillus was given the task of subduing this last pocket of resistance.

The Falerians had taken refuge inside their city walls and Camillus now began a siege. They had, however, prepared for such an eventuality long in advance and were plentifully supplied with food. In fact, they were able to go about their lives pretty much as if everything was normal. The gods continued to receive their sacrifices, entertainment was provided for the citizenry, schools remained open, and every so often families would take walks outside the city walls. The siege went on and on. Sickness broke out among the Romans and their morale sank to a low ebb. Camillus himself began to doubt whether he would ever capture Falerii.

It was in these circumstances that a providential windfall came his way. A Falerian schoolteacher decided he would exploit the current situation to his own advantage. In his care were a number of aristocratic boys, whom he occasionally took on walks outside the city, sticking close to its walls. Little by little, however, he began venturing further and further in the direction of the Roman camp. To distract them, he tested his pupils on important events in Falerian history. The boys suspected nothing. Why would they? They trusted their teacher completely.

One day he led the boys all the way to the Roman line. When they saw soldiers just a hundred paces away, they grew alarmed and were ready to run back to Falerii. The schoolteacher quickly allayed their fears by claiming he had a friend among the Romans whom he wanted to converse with. He would never, he claimed, put their lives at risk. Once they had crossed the line, he informed the guard on duty that he was seeking an audience with Camillus.

'Honoured Roman general', he said, bowing deferentially, when he and his pupils had been conducted into his presence. 'I have a proposition to make to you. These boys are the sons of Falerii's most powerful citizens. I am offering them to you as hostages. Our city is now in your hands. You can use these boys as a lever to gain anything you want. You won't face any more resistance. I leave it up to you to decide what reward this service of mine deserves – I know you to be a man of honour.'

Camillus stared hard at the schoolteacher. 'And this is how you think a man of honour behaves? By making a loathsome deal that puts the lives of innocent children at risk? You're the most despicable person I have ever met. You would actually betray your sacred charge for filthy gain? You're a disgrace to your profession – a profession, let me add, that Romans hold in the highest esteem. Falerii may be my mortal enemy, but I know that Romans and Falerians agree on one thing. We belong to the same human family. Rome is at war with men, not with children. You have brought eternal shame on your city. The stain on its reputation will never be forgotten. Romans conquer their enemies by courage and determination, not by subterfuge and guile.'

Camillus snapped his fingers, whereupon a soldier who was standing at ease sprang to attention. 'Legionary, strip this man of every stitch of clothing he's wearing and tie his hands behind his back', he ordered.

Then he bent down to address the boys, 'I'm going to ask you to do something I would never dream of asking you to do in any other circumstances. Your teacher is a very bad man. You know that know. He has cruelly deceived you and put your lives at risk. I'm going to give each of you a stick and I want you to beat him all the way back to Falerii. Do you think you can do that for me?'

The boys enthusiastically agreed and promptly set about their task with a will. Bloodied and bruised, with huge welts across his back, the schoolteacher was driven back to Falerii. On entering the city, the boys explained his crime to curious bystanders and soon they were being cheered along the way.

THE FALERIAN SCHOOL TEACHER

The Falerian schoolteacher.

This event had profound consequences for the war. When the Falerians found out how nobly Camillus had behaved, their hatred towards the Romans evaporated. A desire to make peace began to gain traction and an ambassador was sent to Rome. When he had been admitted to the Senate, he read out the following message:

'We, the people of Falerii, hereby surrender unconditionally to the Romans. We do so in the belief that you will govern us well. Your esteemed commander, Marcus Furius Camillus, could have chosen an easy victory over us. Instead, he put magnanimity above cruelty, humanity above personal advantage, and honour above ambition. No victory was ever more deserving than the one that you have just won over us. It is a victory over a people who have chosen of their own free will to admit defeat. We in turn affirm our conviction that peace is more powerful than war and that hope is more powerful than hatred. We open our gates to you. We place ourselves at your mercy. We are confident we will never repent our decision.'

It was in this fashion that the Etruscans and the Romans finally laid down their weapons.

Chapter 18

The Gauls Invade

No sooner had the Romans laid aside their differences with the Etruscans than they were placed in mortal peril by the Gauls, a Celtic people whose homeland roughly corresponded to modern day France and Belgium, not to mention Luxembourg, most of Switzerland, northern Italy, part of Germany and the Netherlands.

The Romans had only themselves to blame. They had been warned that trouble was brewing on the horizon. A plebeian called Caedicius had been walking past the Temple of Vesta in the Forum one evening when an eerie woman's voice addressed him.

'Inform the magistrates that the Gauls are coming', the eerie voice said. 'There's no time to lose. Make preparations at once.'

Caedicius nearly jumped out of his skin. He looked all around him, but the streets were completely deserted. Not even a rabid dog was stirring in the shadows. The only plausible conclusion was that the voice had come from inside the Temple of Vesta.

Vesta's temple, situated close to the *regia*, houses Rome's sacred fire. The fire is tended by the Vestal Virgins, whose job it is, as we have seen, to see it never goes out.

The fact that the warning came from such a venerable source naturally made Caedicius feel doubly alarmed.

He ran home literally quaking in his sandals. He couldn't sleep a wink. Well before dawn he hastened to the house of one of the two consuls and banged on the door. Like any patriotic Roman would have done, he felt it was his duty to convey Vesta's warning to the relevant authorities.

The consul wasn't pleased at being woken at such an early hour.

'What on earth is so important that it can't wait till the morning?' he demanded irritably.

Caedicius did his best to give an account of what had happened but kept stumbling over his words.

'You must be stupid', the consul observed contemptuously when he finally understood what Caedicius meant. 'Do you have any idea how far Gaul is from Rome?'

The Temple of Vesta.

Caedicius stared blankly. 'No, I –' he began.

'Just as I thought. And besides, why would you think Vesta would entrust such vital information to you? You're a complete nobody. I don't know what your motive was in coming here today. Perhaps you're one of those halfwits who roam our streets. Or maybe you're doing this to win a bet of some kind. Whatever your motive is, let me warn you, laddie, if you cross my path again, I'll have my lictors beat you black and blue for disturbing the peace. Now get out of here. It's my job to protect honest, hardworking citizens, not to deal with miscreants like yourself.'

'What's a m-m-m-miscreant?'

'Get out!' the consul barked, slamming the door.

The fact of the matter is that Gauls had been living in northern Italy for centuries, but the Romans had been too preoccupied with their neighbours to take any notice of this fact. It's unclear why some of them had left their homeland, but one plausible theory is that they were attracted to Italy because of its wine. The Gauls were already dedicated wine-bibbers, but in this period they were dependent on wine that was produced elsewhere. It wasn't till much later that they started cultivating grapes themselves.

An interesting fact worth mentioning about Gallic soldiers is that they wore trousers, unlike Roman soldiers, who wore short skirts. Well, they didn't actually wear skirts. They wore a tunic, which they slipped over their shoulders and fastened around the waist with a belt. In winter time they wore leggings but these came down only as far down as the knees. Anyway, back to the Gauls. Another interesting fact is that they painted their faces, arms and chests with something called woad before going into battle. Woad is a plant that belongs to the cabbage family. It produces a blue dye. Other than covering themselves in woad, and occasionally performing human sacrifice, the Gauls were fairly civilised, a fact that should not be forgotten.

Sad to say, Vesta's warning thus went unheeded. Soon afterwards a delegation from the Etruscan city of Clusium arrived to inform the Senate that they were being attacked and needed assistance. The Senate was completely taken aback. It had no inkling of the fact that the Gauls were so close. All the same, it decided that Clusium was sufficiently far away not to give immediate cause for alarm. It was also reluctant to get involved in what it regarded as a foreign war.

'Just sit tight', the leader of the Senate told the Clusian delegates. 'We'll send a high-powered embassy to remonstrate with the Gauls. They're bound to come around. I know just the chaps for the job – the Fabii brothers. There are three of them – Quintus, Numerius and Caeso. They'll put these outlandish foreigners in their place in no time flat. We – I mean you – don't have anything to fear.'

The delegates tried to indicate to the Senate that the Gauls were in no mood to be remonstrated with, but to no avail. They therefore had no choice but to head back to Clusium. A few days later the Fabii brothers arrived at the Gallic camp with a cavalry contingent to give the invader a remonstration, as the Senate had promised.

It turned out that the Gallic chief, whose name was Orgetorix, spoke passable Latin, though he adhered to characteristic Gaulish word order, which is the same as English word order, except where Wackernagel's Law applies.

'Look here, laddie', Quintus, the oldest brother, began in an effort to appear friendly. 'I don't know who you are, but I suggest you leave Etruria immediately. The Etruscans haven't done you any harm. I hear you're from the Po Valley. Well, I suggest you go back to the Po forthwith, wherever that is.'

He waited for a response. When none was forthcoming, he continued more assertively, 'And let me give you a warning. We're a peaceful people. We'd prefer to come to terms with you rather than engage in hostilities, but if you don't leave, you'll have to answer to Rome. Romans don't just stand by when their neighbours are attacked.'

'Who did you say you were?' Orgetorix, asked, tugging at an unruly strand of his red beard.

'I didn't. My name is Quintus Fabius Ambustus. I'm the son of Chief Pontiff Marcus Fabius Ambustus.'

'I don't mean your name. I mean the name of your people.'

'We're Romans, duh.'

'Never heard of you.'

'You've never heard of the Romans?' Quintus exclaimed, extending his jaw in disbelief. 'You're kidding.'

'Sorry, no,' Orgetorix replied, languorously plucking a hair from a large mole situated just above his upper lip. 'Anyway, we don't have any grudge against you, whoever you are. We just need a bit of land for our surplus population. I'm sure Clusium can accommodate us without our having to encroach upon you. Just remember, however. All things belong to the brave.'

Then, lapsing into the Gaulish *tengu* or tongue, he added, '*Emmi viros rios ex ria toutia.*'

'What's that supposed to mean?'

'It means I'm a free man from a free land. In other words, watch out, laddie. The Gauls are the most virile people on this earth.'

Quintus was furious. He stormed out of the Gallic camp without another word. Then, without signalling their intent, he and his brothers ordered the troops they had brought with them to prepare for battle. While the Gauls were taking their ease, Quintus mounted his horse, galloped into the Gallic camp at the head of his cavalry, charged at Orgetorix, who happened to be quaffing the local wine from a large two-handled drinking cup with relief decoration depicting the Gallic healing god Borvo performing a sexually explicit ritual of purification, and drove his spear straight through his heart.

I hardly need point out that this was a violation of international law. For an ambassador to kill an enemy chief while on a diplomatic mission – that was the height of inexcusability, irrespective of whether the Gauls were intending to invade Roman territory. It was also an act of utter folly. The Gauls ceased to concern themselves with Clusium and turned all their righteous fury against the Romans.

The Fabii were fully aware of their guilt. However, once they got back to Rome, they began stoking anger against the Gauls by presenting themselves as the injured party. As a result, when the Gauls sent ambassadors to Rome demanding that the Fabii be surrendered to stand trial, the Senate rejected the demand outright. Instead of at least issuing an apology, they added insult to injury by electing all three brothers to the rank of military commanders.

Hearing that their just demand had been rejected, the Gauls rained down curses upon the Romans in the name of their gods Esus, Teutates and Taranis, as well as Rosmerta, Nantosuelta and the aforementioned Borvo. The Fabii, meanwhile, continued to curry favour among their compatriots by seriously underestimating the magnitude of the threat that the enemy posed and by characterising the Gauls as ignorant backwoodsmen, incapable of posing a threat to the might of Rome.

'One day the Gauls will simply melt back into the dark, smelly woods from which they emerged', Quintus claimed. 'I very much doubt they will try to assault our city. And if they do, we'll crush them like cockroaches under our military boots.'

Statements like these always play well with the crowd, but the Gauls didn't disappear into their smelly woods. Less than a month after the events I have described, word reached the Senate that the Gauls were advancing towards Rome at great speed. The Fabii tried to calm the populace by continuing to downplay the threat, but panic had begun to take hold. Eventually it became evident even to the greatest dullard in the land that the Gallic threat had to be taken seriously. It was at this late juncture that the Fabii began scrambling to conscript all able-bodied men into their ranks. Chaos ensued. Towns allied to Rome evacuated their populations and sent them to Rome for protection, causing a chronic food shortage. Wild rumours began to circulate of the terrible acts of barbarism that the Gauls routinely meted out to their foes, such as roasting them on a gridiron.

From the start, things did not go well. The Romans advanced ten miles north till they reached the confluence of the rivers Tiber and Allia. The Gauls were assembled on the further bank with a far larger army than the Romans had been expecting. To add to their dismay, the *modus pugnandi* of the Gauls was unlike that of any enemy the Romans had faced previously. They were chanting discordantly, jeering derisively, sticking their tongues out, and exposing their bare bottoms.

The Fabii were completely unprepared for this kind of reception. To make matters worse, they didn't have the least understanding of basic military strategy. They were completely incompetent. All they could do was draw up their army in an extended battle line, hoping to mask the inferiority of their numbers. The Gallic chief, whose name was Brennus, was not deceived. He instantly understood that the army facing him was no match for his own.

Mars, as the Latin tag has it, was not equal that day. From the moment that the Gauls gave vent to their frightful war cry, panic entered the hearts of the Romans. Once their centre had collapsed, almost all their resistance ceased. The reserves were so terrified merely by the sight of the enemy that they tossed away their shields and fled the field without even attempting to engage in hostilities. Many drowned in the river, some managed to escape back to Rome, others took refuge in Veii. The Battle of the Allia, as it came to be called, was one of the most ignominious days in Roman military history.

The Gauls couldn't believe their luck. They'd never encountered such a pusillanimous enemy before. After decapitating all their prisoners, they tied their severed heads to the wheels of their chariots and sped towards Rome. They got there just as the sun was setting.

Another surprise was awaiting them. The Romans hadn't even bothered to close the gates. No guards stood on duty. No sentries manned the walls. Brennus, being naturally wary, decided to encamp outside the city. He suspected that armed men were lurking in dark corners, ready to ambush his men as soon as they entered the city.

He needn't have worried. The Romans had in effect abandoned Rome.

All Rome, that is, apart from the Capitoline Hill, which Juno had ordered must under no circumstances be abandoned. Accordingly 1,000 able-bodied men with their wives and children withdrew to the hill. Everyone else was left to their fate, including the sick and the elderly.

Those who were able made their escape before the Gauls turned up. They included the six Vestal Virgins. The Vestals knew all too well what fate would await them if they were to remain.

A man of humble origin called Albinus, who was driving his mule cart with his wife and two small boys aboard, happened to observe the Vestals as they were leaving the city. He identified them by their long, thick woollen gowns known as *stolae*, which concealed their forms beneath.

'Unless I'm much mistaken those are the Vestal Virgins', Albinus whispered excitedly to his wife. 'What a disgraceful sight! I'll have to offer them a ride. Get out of the cart, dear, and take the children with you. You don't mind, do you? We'll meet up later. Hurry up. We can't keep them waiting.'

His wife was none too pleased at this, but she didn't want to have a row in front of the Vestals, so she did as her husband bid.

'Excuse me, ladies, but can I offer you a ride?' Albinus asked, once the cart had been vacated, leaning over and patting the seat beside him.

Albinus and the Vestal Virgins.

'You're most kind', the largest of the women, who was evidently the Chief Vestal, replied. 'We gladly accept.'

Albinus was about to offer her his hand but remembered just in the nick of time that it was a capital offence merely to touch a Vestal Virgin. The woman clambered up with difficulty and plonked herself down on the bench beside him, sweat dripping from her armpits. She took up more than half the bench. Fortunately her colleagues were much smaller. One was only six – the youngest age you could become a Vestal Virgin – and two others were barely ten. The six-year-old squeezed herself in between Albinus and the Chief Vestal and the other four climbed in behind. Albinus flicked his whip and his mules slowly set off.

'Where are you heading, reverend one?' Albinus inquired.

'Caere', the Chief Vestal replied.

'Caere?' repeated Albinus, taken aback. 'Caere in Etruria? That's at least thirty miles away. I don't know how much you know about donkeys but their maximum walking speed is about four thousand paces per hour, and they can keep that up for only a short distance. Speedwise a lot depends, of course, on their age, fitness, size, motivation, and, last but not least, what weight they're pulling. These ones aren't spring chickens, that's for sure, and I've never taken them on such a long journey. What with stops for water, I reckon it'll take them about fifteen hours with this load. Sorry, I didn't mean that disrespectfully. We'll have to find a place to stay for the night or perhaps even two nights. Then I've got to turn around and drive the thirty miles back.'

'If you would rather not take us, I'm sure we can find an alternative means of transportation', the Chief Vestal remarked with a sniff, preparing to descend as they came to a crowded intersection.

'Not at all, not at all, reverend mother', Albinus hastily interposed. 'I wouldn't hear of it. I was just thinking aloud. It will be a great honour, a very great honour. I just hope the sacred flame doesn't go out in your absence. That would *not* be a good omen.'

'No worries on that score. The sacred fire is concealed under my *stola.*'

Albinus was about to make a quip but then thought better of it. He flicked his whip across the mules' eyes and slowly they set off, the cart lurching perilously.

Conversation was desultory for the first few miles. Eventually, as the sun began to decline, Albinus decided it was time to break the ice.

'What's it like being a Vestal, if I may inquire?'

'Well, we certainly don't sit around all day long tending the immortal flame, if that's what you think', his companion said tartly, turning to gaze at a line of wooded hills in the distance.

History does not record how Albinus and the Chief Vestal passed the time together as they jostled up and down along a dirt track for the next two days or so, nor whether Albinus came to regret his act of generosity, nor what his wife said to him when he eventually re-connected with his family, assuming he did.

But that is obviously not the point of the story.

Chapter 19

Hard Cheese, Losers!

After camping outside the city following their victory at the Allia River, early the next day the Gauls entered Rome through the Colline Gate on the north-east side of the city. They were completely blown away by the sight that greeted them. They'd never seen temples before and were amazed by their size and magnificence. All they could do was look upwards, open-mouthed and awestruck. Even Brennus was lost for words.

After taking their fill of sightseeing, their thoughts naturally turned to plunder. This they did with some trepidation, still expecting to be attacked at any minute. When they came to the houses of the nobility nestling in the lee of the Palatine Hill, an extraordinary sight met their eyes. The doors of each house were open and inside the atrium was its owner, seated on an ivory throne and dressed in his finest robes. Each resembled a statue of a god, perfectly still and expressionless.

For a while the invaders simply stared open-eyed, overcome with superstitious awe, uncertain whether they were looking at breathing human beings. Finally, one Gaul could bear the tension no longer. Entering the house of a man of advanced years called Marcus Papirius, he gazed at him for a few moments, and then suddenly plucked his silver beard. Instantly Papirius sprang to life. He raised his staff and brought it down on the man's head with all the force at his command. The Gaul gave a yelp, sprang back, drew his sword and thrust it savagely into Papirius' liver.

The spell was now broken and mayhem ensued. It is hardly any exaggeration to say that before long the streets were running with blood. The Gauls rampaged through the city, giving no quarter to anyone. They ransacked houses and set them on fire.

The defenders on the Capitoline Hill looked down helplessly as the massacre took place, both unwilling and incapable of averting it. Such, however, was the piety of the Romans that when it came time to perform an annual sacrifice to Vesta, the Chief Pontiff descended from the Capitol attired in his priestly robes and passed through the ranks of the admiring and dumbstruck Gauls completely unscathed. After discharging his duties, he returned to the Capitol, again unscathed.

For several days and nights fires burned until Rome was little more than a smouldering ruin. Eventually Brennus decided it was time to launch an attack on the Capitoline Hill itself. Discipline in his army was beginning to grow lax and his men were becoming insubordinate. It's a well-known fact that the Gauls, despite their ferocity and valour, are constantly on the point of dissolving into anarchy. Brennus thus gave the signal for the assault to begin.

The defenders were ready for him, however. They waited till the enemy were halfway up the hill and then they launched a counter-attack. Since the hill is extremely steep, the Gauls were driven back and their attack was repulsed.

Brennus now decided to make a night assault on a part of the hill that was unguarded owing to its steep gradient and elevation. A small contingent of crack troops managed to make its way to the summit without being detected. Even the dogs didn't wake up. The Gauls would certainly have succeeded in their objective, had it not been for a vigilant flock of geese. The geese were sacred to Juno Moneta, whose temple was on the northern part of the hill known as the citadel. Juno Moneta protected the public treasury – our word 'money' derives from her cult title. Her temple had been established by Camillus, in fulfilment of his vow after the successful siege of Veii.

As soon as the Gauls gained the rocky ledge leading to the summit of the citadel and were about to jump down onto the terrace below, Juno's geese began whacking them with their wings, biting, and cackling hoarsely. Instantly an officer of the garrison named Marcus Manlius was alerted and hastened in the direction of the cackling. He arrived just as the first assailants were clambering onto the terrace and he ran them through with his sword. Other guards rushed to support him, and the Gallic attack was repulsed.

Next morning the commander of the garrison called his men onto parade to extend his heartfelt thanks to Manlius. He resisted calls to punish *en masse* the guards who had been on duty that night. Instead, he confined his anger to the man in charge, who was punished by being hurled from the Tarpeian Rock. The man could be heard moaning for days, while buzzards and vultures picked at his bones.

Reluctantly the Gauls now settled in for a long siege. Since, however, they'd burned the entire stock of grain when plundering the city without

165

Juno's sacred geese to the rescue.

any thought of how they would survive once it was gone, they were facing starvation. This led to an outbreak of plague. Soon the invaders became so weakened that they didn't have the strength even to bury their dead. The situation wasn't much better on the Capitoline Hill, whose defenders were also short of food, so it wasn't long before the plague spread to them as well.

Though both sides were in a desperate state, the Gauls had the upper hand because at least they could alleviate their hunger by carrying out raids. Finally, the Romans were forced to sue for peace. In requital Brennus demanded the sum of one thousand pounds' weight of gold. This was a huge sum in those days, as it is in these, but such was the extremity of their desperation that the Senate had no option but to agree. It seemed now as if Rome's humiliation was complete.

Worse, however, was to follow. When the gold was being weighed before Brennus, it failed to tilt the scales because the Gauls were using false weights. The Roman commander knew he was being tricked. He stepped forward to register his protest, but Brennus, who was dressed

Brennus tilts the scales.

in goatskin trousers and battered goatskin shoes, shoved him roughly aside. He then threw his sword into the scale with the false weights.

'Hard cheese, losers', he said scornfully, this being a literal translation of the Gaulish phrase he uttered.

Providence, I'm happy to say, sometimes has a way of coming to the rescue, and this is what happened next. Just as Brennus delivered his remark about cheese, Camillus, who had recently been appointed dictator to deal with the crisis, rode into the camp accompanied by the cavalry.

'You're relieved of your duties forthwith', he informed the hapless Roman commander, dismounting from his horse. Then, walking up to Brennus, he announced, 'The deal is off the table. Henceforth Romans will pay you in iron not in gold.'

Brennus looked at his interpreter for clarification.

'What do you mean you'll pay me in iron?' he demanded, when he heard the translation. 'I don't want iron. I want gold. That's the agreement we've made.'

167

'I mean we'll pay you with our swords', Camillus explained haughtily. 'Swords are made of iron.'

Brennus was ready to throw a fit. He accused the Romans of breaking their solemn agreement, but as Camillus had an army at his back, he had to recognise the deal was off the table.

The two armies prepared for battle. On this occasion the Gauls were no match for the Romans and within a short time the tide began to turn against them. The Gauls fled north and then west in the direction of modern-day Luxembourg. Camillus' men were so jubilant that they hailed him 'Rome's second founder' and 'father of his fatherland'.

Despite their victory, this was hardly the moment for the Romans to rest on their laurels. The city no longer faced a threat to its existence, but many buildings had been destroyed, the fortifications were ruined, and the temples were mere shells befouled with excrement.

Again, the populace was so dispirited that a sizeable proportion wanted to abandon Rome and relocate in Veii. Again, it was Camillus who saved the day.

'Are you about to abandon the gods who stood by you in the recent wars?' he demanded of the assembled crowd on the morning when the subject was due to be debated in the Senate. 'Is this how you repay their

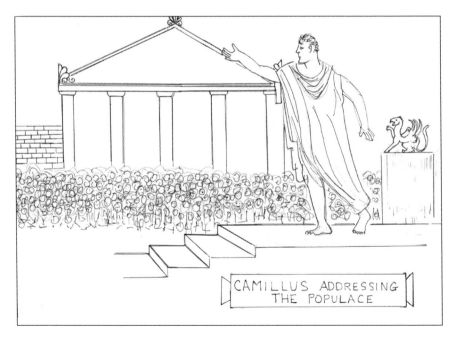

CAMILLUS ADDRESSING THE POPULACE

Camillus addresses the populace.

steadfastness and support? Will Jupiter and Juno cease to be worshipped on the Capitoline Hill? Very well, so be it. But be warned that they won't take your desertion lightly. No longer will you be able to call upon them in your hour of need.'

Camillus produced a lot of other arguments of a more practical nature as to why the Romans should stay put in Rome, but it was the religious argument that won the day – that and an incident that occurred when the Senate began its debate shortly afterwards.

A centurion returning from guard duty with his detachment was passing through the Forum and happened to say to his men, 'OK, lads, we might as well halt here. It's as good a place as any.'

The words 'It's as good a place as any' were overheard and transmitted to the senators, who took them as an omen sent by the gods. A vote was taken and the proposal to relocate to Veii was overwhelmingly rejected. The arduous task of rebuilding Rome began shortly afterwards.

Sadly it was carried out without any overall sense of planning, which is why, in the judgement of the historian Livy, Rome is such a mess.

As soon as the Romans had seen off the Gauls, however, they were faced with a new challenge from the Volscians, now allied with the Latins and a people called the Hernici. The danger was so great that the Senate decided to appoint a dictator to deal with the crisis, a man called Aulus Cornelius Cossus. This in turn created a huge stir because Marcus Manlius, who had grown a bit too big for his boots after saving the Capitol, thought he should have got the job. To gain support, he presented himself as the saviour of the common man. When a centurion was condemned to death for not paying his debts, he made a big show of paying his debts off for him. He then accused the Senate of keeping to itself all the Gallic gold, which it should have distributed among the poor. Cossus had him arrested, but that only made matters worse and when his term as dictator expired, Manlius was released to a great fanfare. He continued to build up his popularity with the plebs, even to the extent of suggesting that he should be granted the title 'champion of the people'.

This gave the Senate the chance it had been waiting for. It accused Manlius of aiming at kingship and put him on trial. He was convicted of treason and condemned to death. The tribunes of the people took him up onto the Capitoline Hill and flung him to his death from the Tarpeian Rock – the very spot from which he had saved Rome from the Gauls.

169

Chapter 20

Sacred Chickens, Et Cetera

It must be apparent by now that Rome's greatness depends not only on the valour and discipline of its army but also on the goodwill and support of its gods, as well as the dead. They are arguably most powerful as the *dii manes*, the dead in divine form. They made an appearance, metaphorically speaking, at the Battle of Mount Vesuvius, the first encounter between the Romans and the Latins in what became known as the Latin Wars.

The night before the battle both consuls, Titus Manlius Torquatus and Publius Decius Mus, had the same dream. They dreamt that victory would only go to the Romans if one of the consuls died in the battle. Next morning, they asked the army soothsayer what they should do.

'There's only one way out. One of you is going to have to perform an act of *devotio* ', the soothsayer informed them.

'What's a *devotio*?' asked Mus, whose name means 'mouse'. There was nothing mousey about Mus, as we'll see.

'It's an extreme *votum*.'

'An extreme vow? What's extreme about it?'

'You vow to sacrifice your life for some cause.'

'Very well, if that's the path to victory, I'm your man', Mus announced. 'I take it there's some sort of prayer you utter?'

'Yes indeed.'

'OK, let's get on with it', said Mus breezily.

'First you need to put on a toga *praetexta* – the one with the purple border.'

Mus quickly removed his armour and slipped on the toga as required.

'Now grasp your chin and stand on your spear. Then repeat after me, "Janus, Jupiter, Mars, Quirinus, Bellona, Lares, and all you gods who hold power over us and our enemies, I beseech you to succour the Roman army in its time of need. I devote all the enemy forces along with myself to the *dii manes* and to Earth."'

Mus repeated the formula, then he and Torquatus gave the order to their troops to prepare for battle. As soon as the two sides engaged, Mus galloped full tilt at the enemy. The Latins were so awestruck by his fearlessness that at first they were rooted to the spot. Then they began hurling their spears at him. Eventually Mus was struck in the neck.

He died instantly. As you would expect, the Latins were heavily defeated.

Torquatus is also celebrated for his service to the Republic. He had killed a Gaul of gigantic proportions by kicking him in the groin. He acquired the name 'Torquatus' because he had ripped off the torque the dead Gaul had been wearing and placed it around his own neck.

There's a tragic side to his story, however. Prior to the commencement of hostilities against the Latins, Torquatus had told his men that it was vital they obeyed his orders because the two sides looked so much alike. This meant *inter alia* that no one was to begin a skirmish on their own because he didn't want Romans killing Romans.

It so happened that Torquatus' son, whose name was also Titus, was riding in some woods one day when he happened to encounter a cavalry commander on the Latin side named Geminus Maecius. Geminus challenged him to single-combat, whereupon Titus, forgetting his father's orders, instantly accepted. Having killed his opponent, he proudly rode into camp, his horse laden with spoils. He was expecting to receive his father's praise for defending the family name. Instead Torquatus ordered him to dismount and roundly berated him for his insubordination. Then in the presence of the entire army he had him beaten to death.

'Let that be a lesson to anyone who thinks of disobeying my orders', Torquatus shouted, not a trace of emotion in his voice.

No sooner had the Romans got the better of the Latins than they found themselves fighting against the Samnites, a people who inhabited south-central Italy. The Samnites had ambushed the Romans at a place called the Caudine Forks, situated between two ravines, and now they had them entrapped.

It was an unusual situation, to put it mildly, and the Samnites found themselves quite at a loss how to proceed. After all, they hadn't actually defeated the Romans and though the incident is referred to as the Battle of the Caudine Forks, this is merely a convention, since the Romans had surrendered to them without offering any resistance. Should they massacre them? Should they enslave them? What in the name of Mamerte – a prominent Samnite deity of indeterminate gender who was the equivalent of Mars – should they do? In the end, they asked Gaius Pontius, their commander-in-chief, to send a letter to his father Herennius for advice. Herennius was judged to be the wisest Samnite alive (and therefore the wisest man in the world).

'Free them all', Herennius wrote back tersely.

When the Samnites read his note, they were completely taken aback.

'That doesn't seem like a very good idea', Pontius' second-in-command remarked. 'What can your father be thinking? Are you sure you explained the situation to him with sufficient clarity, Pontius? He seems a bit confused.'

'Of course I explained the situation to him with sufficient clarity', Pontius sneered. 'He's not confused. He's just being elliptical. That's his style.'

'Well, ellipse or no ellipse, write to him again', the second-in-command urged him.

Pontius shrugged his shoulders and reluctantly consented.

'Kill them', was the reply that came back this time.

Lots of people might have assumed that Herennius was suffering from dementia by this point. Not so the Samnites, a conservative people who deeply respected their elders. Accordingly, they invited Herennius to their war council to explain what he meant.

'It's simple', rasped the old man in his now extinct heavily accented Osco-Umbrian – the language of the Sabines, the Apulians, the Lucanians, etc. – wheezing heavily, a bead of moisture collecting at the end of his hooked nose. 'If you spare the Romans, you'll have their gratitude forever. If you kill them, you'll have peace in the short term, but they'll be back with a vengeance, and you'll suffer accordingly. Do you mean to say you couldn't work that out for yourselves?'

In the end the Samnites opted for a third course of action, which was to humiliate the Romans by stripping them of all their clothing, including their *subligacula*, the Roman equivalent of underpants, and ordering them to pass under a yoke of spears – the same punishment the Romans had meted out to others.

Not long afterwards, however, the Romans, utterly furious at the humiliating treatment they'd received, defeated the Samnites. This was during the Second Samnite War. There was a Third Samnite War, which the Romans also won, after which there was no serious challenge to their leadership in Italy (until 91 BCE, when a lot of people living in the peninsula revolted), other than from abroad.

So, in the end the Romans got their own back, which is pretty much what they have done throughout history and which, I suppose, is the point of the story.

Just as the Romans were about to subdue the whole of southern Italy, a new and alarming threat was presented by a king called Pyrrhus, who ruled a region called Epirus on the north-west coast of mainland Greece. As a child, Pyrrhus had lain awake at night reading about the conquests of Alexander the Great. Once he ascended the throne of Epirus, he decided to model himself upon his predecessor. Instead of directing his attention eastwards as Alexander had done in taking on the might of Persia, however, Pyrrhus turned to the west to take on the might of Rome.

An appeal for support from Tarentum, the most powerful of the Greek colonies, situated in the heel of Italy, gave him the excuse he was looking for. Southern Italy had become so thickly settled by the Greeks that it acquired the name *Magna Graecia*, Great Greece. Their colonies extended along the coast from Capua in the west to Tarentum in the east – a very considerable stretch of territory. Fortunately for the Romans, each *polis* as it was called was autonomous, and though they all shared a similar culture and political set-up they rarely cooperated with one another and did not constitute anything remotely resembling a counterweight to the growing power of Rome.

Borrowing some elephants from his friend and ally Ptolemy II Philadelphus, king of Egypt, Pyrrhus crossed the Adriatic claiming to be on a mission to liberate all the Greeks from Roman oppression. Though victorious in his first battle, it cost him dearly.

'If we win another battle against the Romans, we'll be screwed', Pyrrhus observed in the voiced aspirates of Proto-Indo-European Epirote, which gives us the phrase 'a pyrrhic victory'.

Eventually Pyrrhus returned to Epirus, where, nothing undaunted, he continued his efforts to build an empire of sorts, this time on the Greek mainland. He was killed in the streets of Argos in the Peloponnese. A woman watching from her rooftop hit him with a tile while he was fighting her son, crushing his cervical vertebrae. Plutarch gave him this fitting epitaph: 'Fortune offered him the opportunity to enjoy his wealth without disturbance and to live in peace as king of his own people. But he thought it was nauseating not to be inflicting misery on others or to be suffering misery at the hands of others.'

Thanks to Pyrrhus, Greek independence in Italy had been extinguished, though on the positive side his defeat led to much closer cultural and economic contact between Greeks and Romans.

I hope I've made it clear how vitally important it is to attend to signs sent from the gods. It's especially important to do so before you go into battle. There are many tried and tested ways of discovering what the gods have in store for us, but one failsafe method is to consult sacred chickens. Well, you don't actually consult the chickens, obviously; they don't talk; but you divine the future with their help by either examining their entrails or observing their eating habits. It's a very bad sign if chickens go off their feed because normally they're gobbling all day. So, if a chicken turns up its nose at its feed, you know something is seriously awry. This is exactly what happened during the First Punic War. This was the war that the Romans fought against the Carthaginians, whom they called the *Poeni*. *Poeni* is Latin for 'Phoenicians', hence 'Punic'.

The commander of the Roman fleet during the war was a certain Publius Claudius Pulcher, a descendant of the detestable *decemvir* Appius Claudius. Publius was hardly less detestable.

The morning before he was about to engage the Carthaginian fleet at Drepana, a city on the west coast of Sicily, he instructed his seers to place feed in front of a pair of sacred chickens. To his intense displeasure, the birds showed not the least interest in the feed, despite the fact that they been deliberately starved for days beforehand and hardly had a leg to stand on.

'Bloody sacred chickens', Publius muttered beneath his breath, picking up the sack of grain and emptying its contents in front of them.

As the chickens continued to turn their noses up at the feed, Publius became more and more irate. Eventually he became so frustrated that he seized them by their legs and tossed them far out to sea.

'If you don't want to eat, perhaps you'd like to drink', he jeered, just as Neptune, emitting a single belch, greedily gobbled them down as soon as they hit the corrugated surface of his realm and were eclipsed.

Eclipsed, too, were Publius' hopes. In the ensuing battle the Romans suffered a defeat of catastrophic proportions.

Who said chickens can't foretell the future?

Eventually, however, the Romans won the First Punic War, as a result of which they became the leading power in the Central Mediterranean.

CHICKEN REJECTING
CHICKEN FEED

Sacred chickens foretell the future.

Scarcely a generation passed before they were engaged in the Second Punic War. You'll recall that Dido, queen of Carthage, had cursed Aeneas long ago when, at Jupiter's command, he abandoned her. The avenger she had called for now materialised in the person of Hannibal Barca, arguably Rome's most formidable opponent. On attaining manhood in the immediate aftermath to the First Punic War, Hannibal was consumed from childhood with a burning hatred for Rome. Legend has it that his father had made him swear an oath of eternal animosity on the altar of the Phoenician god Ba'al. Once he grew up, the young man determined to make good his oath.

Hannibal set out on his journey to Italy from Carthago Nova, New Carthage, in Spain with an army that included thirty-seven elephants. Having successfully crossed the Alps just as winter was coming on, he defeated the Romans in three major battles. His greatest victory was at Cannae in southeast Italy, where the Romans lost 50,000 men. That was arguably more casualties than any western army has suffered since in a single day.

'If you give the order to march on Rome, you'll dine on the Capitol in five days', his cavalry commander Maharbal told him in the characteristically nasalised fricatives of Phoenicio-Punic.

Hannibal crosses the Alps.

'I'll pass', Hannibal replied sibilantly. 'But thanks all the same.'

'You know how to win a battle, but you do not know how to make use of it', Maharbal declared ruefully, chewing thoughtfully on his labiodentals.

Even though they had vastly outnumbered the Carthaginians, the Romans should have known they were on a hiding to nothing. A few months earlier a couple of Vestal Virgins had been convicted of breaking their vow of chastity. One had been buried alive, the other had committed suicide.

Following his victory, Hannibal ordered the removal of the gold rings from the fingers of all the dead senators and knights. He put the rings in a basket to indicate the scale of his victory and sent it to the Carthaginian Senate with a request for reinforcements.

The Senate declined his request.

Three years later, Hannibal encamped outside Rome's walls. Panic reigned in the city. Women fled to the temples, sweeping the altars with their hair in a gesture of abject supplication. Hannibal

Coin depicting the head of Hannibal.

rode up to the Colline Gate in the north to inspect the defences and the next day he drew up his army in line of battle. The Romans followed suit with what forces they could muster after their losses at Cannae. Fortunately for them, however, a torrential downpour occurred, which prevented the two armies from engaging. Both sides decided to pack it in for the day. As soon as the Carthaginians got back to their camp, however, the clouds dispersed and the sun came out. The following day Hannibal offered battle again. Again the Romans accepted, but again a torrential downpour occurred, followed by a blue sky once the Carthaginians retreated. It became obvious to Hannibal that the gods were protecting Rome and he never threatened Rome again.

He remained in the Italian peninsula, looting and destroying crops, for three more years. It seemed to the Romans that they would never be shot of him. To make matters worse, Rome was plagued with a variety of prodigies, including meteor showers, pigs being born with human heads, famine, hailstones consisting of blood, etc., etc. This could mean only one thing. Some catastrophic event was going to occur unless appropriate steps were taken to

177

avert it. But what steps? The only thing to do was to consult the Sibylline Books, three of which, you'll recall, were preserved from the original nine. The Senate instructed the Chief Pontiff and all the minor pontiffs to thumb through the scrolls and come up with an answer, which they did.

'We need to introduce the Great Mother', the Chief Pontiff declared.

'How do we do that? Doesn't the Great Mother live in Phrygia?' a senator demanded.

'She does indeed, but Phrygia is where Pergamum is, and Pergamum is our ally', the Chief Pontiff replied.

So the Romans immediately sent a ship to bring the Great Mother to Rome.

Throughout their history the Romans have always been welcoming foreign gods, whose arrival takes the form of the ceremonial entry of a statue or other object associated with the deity in question.

The Great Mother eventually sailed into the port of Ostia at the mouth of the River Tiber. An entourage of Roman worthies was waiting on the shore to greet her. However, as it headed towards the quay, the ship that was transporting her ran aground on the shallows. An army of slaves was promptly dispatched into the water to tow it to land but, heave as they might, they were unable to dislodge the ship from its resting place. She wasn't called the *Great* Mother for nothing, it turned out.

It was then that a miraculous event took place. A woman called Claudia Quinta had been falsely accused of adultery. Though she had vehemently denied the charge, a cloud hung over her head and she was publicly shunned. Claudia had witnessed the plight of the Great Mother and saw a heaven-sent opportunity to clear her name.

'O Great Mother', Claudia prayed earnestly, 'you who inhabit the mountains of Phrygia, you who cause your celebrants to engage in ecstatic dancing, if I am guiltless of adultery, endow me with the strength to bring you to safe ground.'

The goddess heard her prayer and Claudia achieved what men had failed to achieve. She tied the ship's rope to her belt and with superhuman strength heaved the ship out of the sandbar. Henceforth she was honoured as a shining example of chastity. It all goes to show.

This was not all, however. What the dignitaries had been expecting was a statue of the Great Mother in human form. Instead, what was

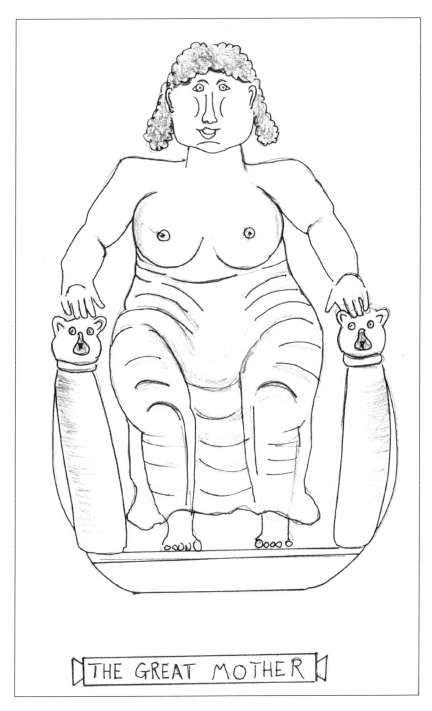

The Great Mother.

CLAUDIA QUINTA'S HEROIC ACT

Claudia Quinta's heroic act.

transported down the gangplank was a large black meteorite. The meteorite was accompanied by long-haired castrated priests wearing lots of bling, who, with castanets, cymbals, tambourines and drums, were producing a tumult of discord, while with their free hands were indulging in a ritual of self-flagellation.

'Oh well', the dignitaries thought. 'We can hardly send it – her – back after all the palaver of getting her here in the first place.'

Despite their misgivings, the goddess did her job, and Hannibal withdrew from Italy. The next year he was defeated at Zama, a town five days west of Carthage. The Roman commander, Publius Cornelius Scipio, was awarded the title 'Africanus' in commemoration of his stunning victory. He had used Hannibal's elephants against him by causing them to panic and trample the Carthaginian ranks.

Sicily, Sardinia, Corsica and Spain now fell to Rome.

Women don't feature prominently in Republican Rome, but one who did, at least posthumously, was Scipio's daughter Cornelia. Cornelia achieved star status by being an exemplary wife and mother; or, as we might say, by acquiescing in the gender-stereotyping of her day. She had married a man much older than herself called Tiberius Sempronius

Gracchus, by whom she had twelve children. When he died, she remained loyal to his memory, even going so far as to reject an offer of marriage from Ptolemy VIII, nicknamed *Physkon* or 'Fatso'. Cornelia was also famed for inspiring, or perhaps nagging would be a more accurate word, two of her sons, Tiberius and Gaius, to make a name for themselves in politics. Both became tribunes of the plebs and initiated important social reforms, and both died as a result, having aroused the ire of the Senate.

An interesting story is told of Gracchus' head. His fellow tribune and sworn enemy, Lucius Opimius, had announced that he would pay in gold the weight of Gracchus' head to the person who delivered it to him. A certain Septimuleius produced it. When placed in the scales, it was found to weigh a staggering seventeen and two-thirds pounds. The average head weighs between eight to twelve pounds. Opimius smelt a rat. He ordered the head to be examined by a Greek physician.

'Hello, hello', the physician said, poking at the skull with his scalpel and forceps. 'What's this? I do believe some blighter has removed the brain and poured in what very much looks like solidified molten lead.'

Opimius was scandalised. He summoned Septimuleius and gave him the equivalent of a right royal bollocking. Then picking up Gracchus' head he hurled it at Septimuleius' head. It struck him between his eyes, flattening his nose. He died instantly.

Back to the enmity between Rome and Carthage. Such was the terror which Hannibal had aroused that many decades later a crusty old figure called Cato the Censor ended every speech he delivered with the words, 'Carthage should be destroyed.' A censor was a magistrate who scrutinised public morals. He also maintained the census, the equivalent of a voting register, which was complicated by the fact that the citizenry was divided up into property-owning classes.

Half a century later Carthage was indeed destroyed. Legend has it that the city housed half a million inhabitants. After the Romans had done with it, only 50,000 survived, who were sold into slavery. This, in other words, was an act of genocide.

Venomous old Cato didn't live long enough to see his dream come true. He'd died two years earlier.

Incidentally, Cato didn't have much time for omens. A man once came to him asking him what might be the significance of the fact that mice had been gnawing on his shoes. Cato wittily or perhaps astringently replied, 'It might mean something if the shoes had been gnawing on the mice.'

Hannibal cast a long shadow on the Romans, who never forgot how close they'd come to being annihilated. Mothers would discipline their disobedient children with the warning, 'Hannibal is at the gates!'

After seeing off the Carthaginians, the Romans saw off the Greeks, first the Greeks who lived in mainland Greece, and then the Seleucid Greeks who inhabited Syria and parts of Turkey in territory that was a remnant of the empire of Alexander the Great.

The story goes that, when the Seleucid king Antiochus IV Epiphanes, 'God made manifest', was on his way to lay siege to Alexandria in Egypt, he was met by a Roman ambassador called Gaius Popillius Laenas. Laenas presented Antiochus with a directive from the Senate. The directive ordered him to withdraw from Egypt forthwith.

'Forthwith?' the king repeated, trying to sound casual. 'Let me think about this. I'll need to discuss it with my council. I'll get back to you tomorrow.'

He turned and was about to leave when Laenas picked up a stick and drew a circle in the sand around him.

'You're not to move out of this circle until you tell me what I'm to say to the Senate', Laenas said sharply.

Antiochus' jaw dropped a mile.

'I – I obey', he eventually stammered.

Laenas extended his hand in friendship and slapped Antiochus on the back.

It was thus, by drawing a circle in the sand, that the Romans eventually acquired the Seleucid Empire.

Up till now the Roman army was a conscript army. Only male citizens who met a strict property requirement could serve. They were paid a pittance and mostly depended on plunder. As a result of these restrictions, the army was stretched beyond its limits. Gaius Marius, seven times consul, changed all that. As a child, he had discovered an eagle's nest with seven eggs in it. Eggs are sacred to Jupiter so it was clearly an omen of great things to come, and he later realised that it could only mean one thing – that he would hold the consulship seven times. He later decreed that the eagle should be Rome's symbol par excellence.

Marius' most important reform was to permit men who owned no property to serve in the Roman army. Henceforth the state provided all soldiers with government issue arms and armour. No longer were soldiers recruited at the beginning of the campaigning season. Instead Rome now had a standing army. Veterans received a retirement package, which included a parcel of land. As a result of these reforms Marius defeated huge tribes of Gauls and Teutons, who were invading Italy. There was, however, a fatal flaw in the system he set up: on completion of service, legionaries looked to their commander for land to settle, and the allegiance legions owed to their commanders and the need of those commanders to provide their veterans with land was a major cause of the breakdown of the Republic.

This came to a head in the opposition between Marius and Lucius Cornelius Sulla. Marius presented himself as the champion of the poor, whereas Sulla wanted to safeguard the interests of the Senate. Though at the beginning of his career Sulla served under Marius, they first fell out and later became deadly enemies. When Sulla was given the command to go out east and wage war against Mithridates VI, king of Pontus, modern-day northeastern Turkey, Marius got the Senate to reverse its decision and appoint him instead. Sulla marched on Rome, proving that legionaries were now loyal to an individual and not to the Republic, and Marius fled the city.

A word about Mithridates, a wily old fox, who defeated the Romans in many battles. To avoid being poisoned he consumed arsenic, strychnine and cyanide – anything he could get his hands on from the many-venomed earth – to build up resistance in his body, gradually increasing the dose to achieve immunity. He lived to fight another day, actually many other days, after Sulla departed from the east. He died at a very advanced age – well, very advanced for those days – at 74. He was one of the biggest thorns in the side of the Romans.

After making an agreement with Mithridates, Sulla marched on Rome for the second time. Marius had died but thousands still supported his cause. This time around, the Tiber overflowed its banks, choked with the bodies of his slain enemies. The severed heads of his most hated foes became ornaments in his home. Marius' corpse was disinterred and torn to pieces. Sulla assumed the title *Felix*, 'Lucky', recalling what an old woman had said to his parents many years ago: 'Your boy will bring luck both to you and to the Republic.' He assumed the post of dictator, which no one had held for 120 years, but not for just six months; he resigned two years later to write his memoirs, the first politician in history so to do. He'd received a prophecy that he would die at the height of his power; perhaps he thought he could evade it by retiring from public office. Worms chewed on his intestines or else he died of alcohol abuse. 'No better friend, no worse enemy' was his own epitaph.

When Sulla first captured Rome, he had exercised restraint and executed only one of his enemies, Publius Sulpicius Rufus, a tribune of the plebs, whom a slave betrayed. Sulla hated the tribunate, which served as a check to the Senate, and removed many of its powers when he became dictator.

He awarded the slave his freedom and immediately after had him hurled from the Tarpeian Rock for betraying his master, such was Sulla.

LUCIUS CORNELIUS SULLA

Lucius Cornelius Sulla.

Slaves have hardly featured in this account, but they've been there all the time, keeping the wheels turning. Without their input, not to mention their suffering and sacrifice, Rome would never have become great. They shouldn't be an endnote, given their vast importance and sheer numbers,

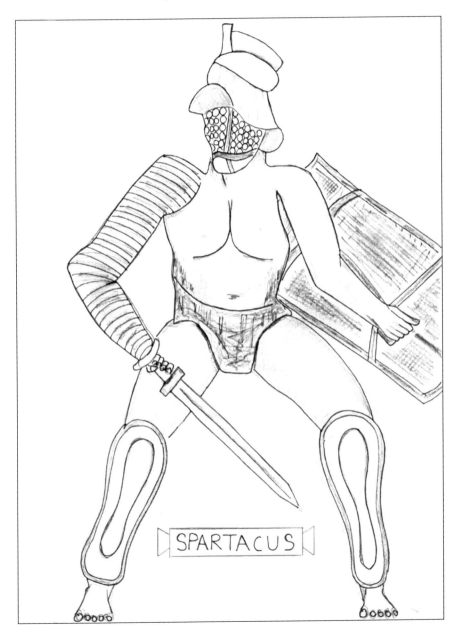

Spartacus.

but that's all they can be in a book on Roman legends. They briefly enter our story when about fifty highly-trained gladiators break out of their training camp in Capua in southern Italy after grabbing whatever they can from the kitchens to serve as weapons. After plundering the region around Capua, they take up a defensible position on Mount Vesuvius. Before long they have attracted tens of thousands of supporters and sympathisers, many of them impoverished and dispossessed citizens, including a large number of discontented veterans.

It wasn't the rebels' intention to overthrow the institution of slavery. No one in the ancient world advocated for that, not even Jesus. Slavery was an inescapable fact of life, no different from Roman sovereignty over the Mediterranean and beyond, another inescapable fact of life. The slaves just wanted freedom for themselves, while the dispossessed and disgruntled Romans just wanted a better life.

Spartacus succeeded in holding the Romans at bay for two years, winning a number of victories. Eventually, however, the rebels were overwhelmed in a region down south called Lucania, modern-day Basilicata. Most of them were killed, including Spartacus, whose body was never found. The survivors – perhaps some 6,000 in all, but no one was counting – were crucified along the Appian Way, the road that led from Rome to Capua, one hanging body every twenty-two paces.

Chapter 21

The Die is Cast!

The Republic eventually came to an end because ambitious generals were putting their own interests before the good of the state. Creaking under the weight of its own inadequacies, it was no longer able to function within the rules and guidelines that had been laid out four hundred years earlier. It had been established to run a city. It now ran an empire. That empire extended from the Straits of Gibraltar to the Euphrates River. It included Spain, southern France, Sicily, Corsica and Sardinia, the coastline of former Yugoslavia, Macedonia, Greece, western Turkey and Tunisia.

If the breakdown of the Republic should be laid at the door of any one man, that man was Caius Julius Caesar. Caesar was without question the most gifted man of his generation – perhaps of any generation. His mental agility was such that he could dictate four different letters to four secretaries simultaneously. His physical quiddities included the ability to gallop sitting backwards on his horse.

Caesar came to power by making a secret deal, known as the Triumvirate, with Crassus and Pompey, the two most powerful men of their day. Though Crassus and Pompey had been enemies, they shared one thing in common: the Senate had refused to pass legislation in their favour. By means of bribery and corruption they got Caesar elected consul so that he could legislate in their favour. To seal the deal Pompey married Caesar's daughter Julia. Once elected, Caesar intimidated his consular colleague, even getting his henchmen to empty a bucket of excrement over his head. The Senate failed to intervene, awarding Caesar a five-year command over Gaul.

The Gallic War, which Caesar ended up waging for eight years, was exceedingly bloody. Gaul was the largest piece of real estate the Romans ever acquired in one go. One million Gauls died and one million were taken captive. After the final battle Caesar ordered the hands of all the prisoners to be cut off and then dispersed them (the men, that is, not the hands) through the province to inspire dread among those who might be plotting insurrection.

Caesar's most notable action, however, was to follow in the wake of Sulla by crossing at the head of his army the Rubicon, a little stream in the north of Italy which marked the legal limit of his authority and where a general was supposed to separate himself from his men. It was here that he uttered the famous words 'the die is cast' and initiated the Civil War, which he won against his rival Gnaeus Pompeius Magnus or, as he is more popularly known, Pompey the Great. He took this action in response to the passing of 'the last decree of the Senate', which left him exposed to legal challenges. As he commented prophetically to his officers on the banks of the Rubicon, 'Friends, to leave this stream uncrossed will breed much trouble for me. To cross it, much trouble for all mankind.'

It was, as he knew, a huge gamble.

You wouldn't exactly call Caesar handsome, though there was something arresting about his features, which lent them a hypnotic effect. His face was weather-beaten – the result of eight years of campaigning in Gaul, where he served as proconsul. His complexion was fair, his nose bulbous, his cheeks sunken, and his neck scraggy, with a few thick white hairs poking out horizontally. He had a depression running from his forehead to his crown, which suggested that he had in some encounter been severely bludgeoned with a blunt instrument. He was bald apart from the sides of his head and a few remaining hairs which he assiduously brushed forward from his temples. His most striking feature were his jet-black eyes, which periodically settled on you with an intensity that could make you almost jump out of your skin. He was of athletic build and, at five feet six inches tall – an excellent height – rather taller than the average Roman.

No principles were at stake in the Civil War, despite the fact that those who supported Pompey claimed to be defending the Republic. In reality both men were motivated by self-interest. Both were intensely competitive, and thousands died in consequence. What made the conflict all the more painful was that it was intrafamilial. Pompey had been married to Caesar's daughter Julia, a woman famed for her beauty and intelligence, and had loved her deeply. She had died giving birth, as was all too common back then, before the rupture between her father and her husband had become inevitable.

The definitive battle took place at Pharsalus in Thessaly, northern Greece. Caesar was outnumbered by over two to one. 15,000 Pompeians

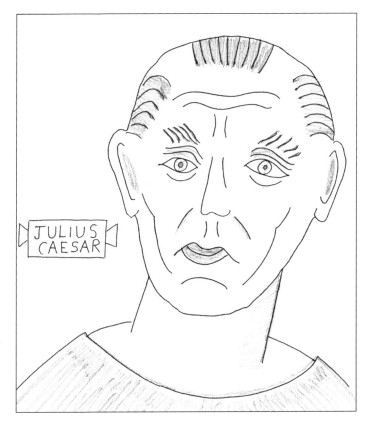

Julius Caesar contemplates the empire's many problems.

A Roman battle line.

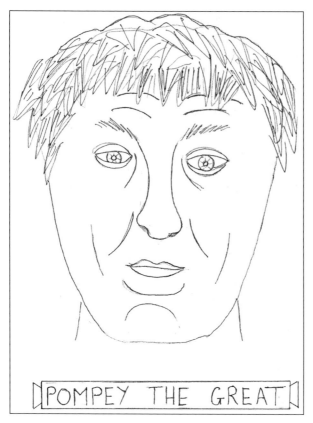

Pompey the Great.

The Battle of Pharsalus.

perished in the battle, compared with only 200 Caesarians. *Hoc voluere*, 'This is what they wanted', was Caesar's famous pronouncement, as he viewed the carnage, acquitting himself of all responsibility.

Pompey fled to Alexandria in Egypt. As soon as he stepped on shore, he was murdered on the orders of the Pharaoh Ptolemy XIII. Ptolemy no doubt thought he was doing Caesar a favour. However, when Pompey's signet ring was brought to him as proof that his rival was dead, Caesar wept. He declined to be shown his severed head.

Caesar now began an affair with the twenty-one-year-old Cleopatra VII Philopator, Ruler of the Two Lands of Egypt, High Priestess of Every Temple, Bearer of the Rods of Horus, etc., etc., as she later became. She was thick-browed, had green eyes with long dark lashes, a freckled, hooked nose, and full red lips. Caesar always felt a quickening of the pulse, a heave in the chest, in the presence of an attractive woman. She was being besieged by her brother/husband Ptolemy. Legend has it that she was smuggled into the palace where he was residing wrapped in a carpet.

The murder of Pompey.

Having installed Cleopatra on the throne of Egypt as joint ruler with her brother, Caesar hastened to Syria, where he defeated Pharnaces II, king of a client kingdom known as Pontus on the southern shore of the Black Sea. Pharnaces had been unsuccessfully trying to break away from Rome. *Veni, vidi, vici*, 'I came, I saw, I overcame', Caesar pronounced at the end of his lightning campaign.

I can't resist telling an anecdote about Cleopatra that dates to the period of her relationship with Mark Antony some years later. One evening, when Antony was gorging himself as usual, Cleopatra wagered

Cleopatra.

that she was prepared to spend ten million sesterces on a single banquet. Antony took on the bet and next evening she set before him an extravagant meal, though not costlier than its predecessor. When Antony belittled it, she called for the second course. This turned out to be a small vessel containing sour vinegar. Cleopatra removed her priceless pearl earrings and casually dropped them into the vinegar, with the result that they liquefied immediately. She then swallowed the contents of the vessel in one gulp, declaring herself to be the winner.

Even after the death of Pompey, the Civil War continued to rage. Hostilities moved to modern-day Tunisia, where Caesar defeated the Pompeians at Thapsus. After the battle, his men exacted savage revenge by killing all their prisoners, who were of course their fellow citizens, despite Caesar's repeated command to spare them. He wasn't at his best that day, having had an epileptic seizure, to which he was prone, so that was why his men ran amok. Caesar himself was famed for his clemency. It was an attribute that placed him on the same footing as the gods.

When Marcus Porcius Cato, commander of the garrison at Utica some fifty miles away, learned of the defeat, he realised the Republican cause was lost. He chose to commit suicide in preference to humbling himself by becoming the recipient of Caesar's clemency. Cato was an adherent of the Stoic school of philosophy, which exalted death as the guarantor of personal freedom. The Stoics saw suicide as an honourable way out of an intolerable existence, whether due to physical pain, abject misery or political oppression.

Cato is alleged to have spent his last night reading Plato's dialogue *Phaedo* on the immortality of the soul. When he finished, he picked up a dagger and thrust it into his belly, hitting a major artery. He sank back onto his bed, barely conscious. However, his groans alerted his slaves, who rushed in and attempted to bandage up the wound. Cato summoned the last particle of his strength and tore off the dressing. Then he ordered his slaves out of the room. Minutes later he expired. He was the most principled of the Pompeians, the only one who believed in the common good, and with his death republicanism came to an end.

Following his victory at Thapsus, Caesar was elected dictator for ten years. He now made it his priority to introduce a raft of administrative reforms touching on virtually every aspect of Roman life. First day on the job he summoned his secretary:

CATO

Cato, the diehard
Republican.

'Things in Rome have been going to rack and ruin during Caesar's absence in Africa, Spain and elsewhere', he began, referring to himself in the third person as was customary. 'The Civil War has destroyed the social fabric. There's a need for widespread reform. For starters, there are far too many Romans on the dole. The dole encourages idleness. We have to reduce the number of recipients, but in a way that is even-handed. Not all the claimants are malingerers. Some are, some aren't. There are the veterans, for a start. You'll agree they have a perfect right to a handout, even the ones who fought on Pompey's side. Caesar doesn't discriminate. Let bygones be bygones, that's always been his motto. Forgive and forget. We're all one big happy family now. In short we'll need to establish criteria of eligibility for the dole, which means we'll have to conduct a census of the entire populace.

'Talking of the populace, in case you haven't noticed, Rome is bursting at the seams. There isn't enough housing to go around. No wonder there are so many beggars. Reducing the size of Rome's population is Caesar's number one priority. Well, one of his number one priorities. It's up there, in other words. One way to do this is by founding new colonies – in Italy, obviously but also in Spain, Gaul, Greece, Syria, the Black Sea region, et cetera, et cetera. At the same time, Caesar wants to encourage professionals to settle in the capital. Rome is suffering from a chronic shortage of doctors and teachers. We need more Greeks. They make the best teachers and doctors. I know there's a lot of prejudice against Greeks – lots of people think you can't trust them – but they're damned clever chappies, a damned sight cleverer than your average senator, that's for sure.

'The Republic – we're going to go on calling it a republic even though Caesar is a dictator for life – no longer has the resources to meet the demands of our expanding empire. Take our Forum to begin with. It ran out of office space yonks ago. We'll need to build a new one. We'll call it the Julian Forum – after me. I've got surveyors already working on a plan. It'll include a temple to my great-great-great-great-great-grandmother Venus Genetrix, Venus the Mother.

'Another thing. We're having to import more and more grain for our ever-growing population, not to mention other foodstuffs, plus raw materials, merchandise, and whatnot. The port of Ostia at the mouth of the River Tiber is going to have to be dredged so that it can accommodate larger vessels. It'll take an army of slaves, but it has to be done, and done fast. We also need to come up with a more efficient system of unloading cargo so that the stuff doesn't rot in the ships. If we don't, we'll all be screwed, if you'll pardon my Gallic. Caesar is working on a plan right now. It's the multiplier effect, you see. Once you get a balls-up here, you get a balls-up squared.

'Then there's the problem of the Pomptine marshes to the south of Rome. They stink to high heaven and they're a dreadful health hazard, particularly in the mosquito season. They'll have to be drained. This means laying endless miles of terracotta piping. Come to think of it' – here Caesar paused and began making rapid jottings in a large roll that lay on the table in front of him – 'we might actually be able to kill two peacocks with one stone by building settlements on the reclaimed land.

'We've also got to do something about the calendar. It's in an infernal mess. It's a symbol of the disorder and chaos into which Rome has sunk. We had to intercalate numerous months last year to get it back into alignment with the solar year. But this will be the *annus ultimus confusionis,* you can bet your bottom obol on that. Caesar will get a Greek to sort it out and then – bingo! – no more bloody intercalation ever again. We'll call it the Julian calendar.

'Talking about Greeks, Caesar is all for ethnic diversity – Sarmatians, Dacians, Bactrians, Egyptians, Armenians, Carpathians, Numidians, Cappadocians and Jews – don't forget the Jews, Caesar's favourites – not to mention Sugambrians, Venetians, Venellians, Aeduans, Bellovacians, Arvenians, Sequanians, Atuacians – you name it the more, the merrier. Rome is a huge melting pot and all the better for it. We've always been a mixed bunch, right from the word go. Our founding fathers, you'll recall, when they fled from the ashes of Troy under the leadership of Father Aeneas, intermarried with the Latins as soon as they arrived in Italy. It was the only way to prevent the line from fizzling out. Then later under Father Romulus they abducted Sabine women when they were experiencing a manpower crisis. You know all this, I take it? You've studied history? Foreigners are the lifeblood of our nation, always have been, always will be.

'Next there's the issue of public morals. People are spending billions of *denarii* on fancy clothing, flashy jewellery, lavish meals, and garish funerary monuments. Far too many of them are taking a litter instead of walking these days. It's a damned disgrace. Exercise is what got Rome to where she is today. We used to be a nation of hardy little subsistence farmers, but we're turning into a nation of weaklings. Before you know what's what, the barbarians will be banging at our gates. They'll have us for their sandal straps, you mark my words. Those patrician johnnies are the worst offenders. Idle sods, the lot of them, and you can quote Caesar on that. If the patricians don't set an example, how can you expect the plebs to toe the line?

'Talking of transportation, our roads need to be improved. They're falling into disrepair. Roads are the cement that holds our empire together, the vital arteries that pump the blood of our civilization to its uttermost extremities. If we don't maintain them in tip-top condition, the empire will simply fall apart.

'We also need to encourage loafers back onto the land. They've all fetched up in Rome. It's an age-old problem that goes back three generations to the time when Tiberius Gracchus was tribune of the plebs. Tiberius tried to solve the urban overpopulation crisis by handing out parcels of land to the poor and dispossessed. But that was only a stop gap solution. It's the demographic shift to the city that's the root cause of our social decay. Families are disintegrating and morality is crumbling about our ears. We've got to do something about it damn quick.

'And another thing. There are some very dubious beliefs about the afterlife circulating around these days. All sorts of crazies are claiming that happiness exists in some other world rather than in the here and now. Load of old cobblers if you ask Caesar. It'll be the kiss of death to Rome if that idea ever starts to gain ground. I'm a solid Epicurean myself. Death is, death is' – here, Caesar paused pregnantly to allow the full weight of his insight to sink in – 'death. Enjoy life to the full, because there's nothing to come after. To the crows with all those quasi-religio-crypto-nihilistic outfits that question Rome's fitness to rule the world.

'Anyway, the long and the short of it is that Rome is facing a crisis or rather many crises. It's all due to the civil war, as I said. If Pompey had been prepared to negotiate with me, we wouldn't all be in this pickle now. No point rehashing ancient history, however. The point is that the civil war undermined Rome politically morally, socially and economically. There's so much work to do, so little time.'

Even after the Battle of Thapsus, peace remained as elusive as ever and about ten months later Caesar left for Spain to quell a revolt that was led by Pompey's sons, Gnaeus and Sextus. The battle was by no means a foregone conclusion. 'I've fought for my honour many times', Caesar remarked, 'but only now for my life.' Legend has it that he covered the 1,350 miles to his military headquarters at Obulco in twenty-seven days. If this is true, it means his army averaged over fifty miles per day. He defeated Gnaeus and Sextus at the Battle of Munda in southern Spain.

In September 45, about six months after the Battle of Munda, Caesar wrote his will. He left three-quarters of his estate to the grandson of his sister Julia, Caius Octavius, aged eighteen, who was destined to become the Emperor Augustus. He also adopted Octavius as his official heir. If the great man had done nothing else in his life, this act alone would have been enough to change the course of Roman – and indeed – world history.

Over the course of several weeks Caesar celebrated a quadruple triumph – the most magnificent event of its kind ever held. It was in honour of his victories in Gaul, Egypt, the Black Sea region and North Africa. The main exhibit at the Gallic triumph, which was the most spectacular of the four, was Vercingetorix, the chief of the Arverni. Vercingetorix, who united many Gallic tribes under his standard, had led a rebellion after Caesar had all but pacified Gaul. The great man never forgave him. He incarcerated his enemy in Rome's underground prison known as the *Carcer*, access to which could be gained only by a shaft

Vercingetorix.

that was enclosed with iron bars. Its walls oozed with the slime of ages and the screams of its inmates were enough to drive the most stoically self-disciplined insane. There he remained for five years, merely to be led in triumph at Caesar's victory parade.

What must it have been like for him finally to emerge into the blinding sunlight?

After the parade Vercingetorix was led away to be garroted – a slow and agonising death more painful than waterboarding.

Inmates in the *Carcer*.

Chapter 22

The Ides of March

The final three months of Caesar's life proceeded with an inexorable momentum. He was finding it more and more difficult to control his temper and becoming more and more high-minded in his dealings with the Senate. His friends had deserted him, and his hearing was failing. The presence of Cleopatra, whom he hosted on his estate on the Janiculum Hill, added fuel to the rancour that many felt towards him.

Our last sighting of Caesar before his assassination is at the Lupercalia, the festival which took place in the middle of February. As we saw earlier, half-naked youths ran around the Palatine Hill, striking women to make them fertile. Mark Antony, a consul and Caesar's close friend, used the occasion to offer him a diadem, the symbol of kingship. When he did so, the populace began booing, suspecting this to be an attempt to crown Caesar as king. Caesar refused it. Antony offered it again, whereupon he refused it a second time. After he had refused it a third time, he ordered Antony to deposit it in the Temple of Jupiter Best and Greatest. At this the populace broke into thunderous applause.

Was this a fake coronation orchestrated jointly by Caesar and Antony, or was it a charade cooked up by Caesar's enemies and intended to discredit him? The jury is still out.

A day or so later Caesar was approached by a soothsayer called Spurinna, a thin balding man of advanced years with thick lips and large, unsightly canines that projected from his mouth even when it was closed tight.

'Beware the Ides of March', Spurinna warned ominously.

'The man's a dreamer', Caesar remarked nonchalantly, tossing a few coins at his feet.

On the morning of his death, just before he entered the Senate House, he encountered Spurinna a second time.

'Well, the Ides have come', Caesar observed with a light laugh.

'Yes, but they haven't gone', Spurinna quipped somberly.

Caesar had previously ignored a warning that morning from his wife Calpurnia. She had dreamt that the roof of the *regia*, where they resided, had collapsed and that she had been cradling her husband in her arms, while his body spouted jets of blood.

He was the victim of a vast conspiracy, involving perhaps as many as eighty senators. He fell, aptly one might say, at the foot of a statue of Pompey the Great in a public building that Pompey had donated to the state. His assassins had hidden their daggers in small boxes that

Calpurnia reflects upon her husband's infidelities.

contained their copies of the agenda for the upcoming meeting of the senate. There were no security checks back then.

When Marcus Brutus, one of the ringleaders of the conspiracy, stabbed him, Caesar gasped and said, in Greek, 'You, too, child'. It was, as Shakespeare phrased it, the unkindest cut of all. He now ceased to defend himself and fell heavily to the ground. It was a botched job. Some of the assassins slipped and fell in the victim's blood, others were wounded by their co-conspirators.

Caesar's use of the word 'child' was suggestive, since it implied that the crime was one of parricide. Technically this was correct, as Caesar had recently been awarded the title 'father of the fatherland'. More suggestively, there was also a rumour that he was Brutus' biological father through his relationship with Brutus' mother Servilia. It is thus possible that Caesar's remark was doubly *au point*.

The Ides of March.

As he lay gasping his last, a Greek friend of his called Artemidorus, hearing what had happened, had run to his side and caught his last words. Shedding his official persona, Caesar now lapsed into the first person:

'Though it's impossible to imagine what the world would be like without our civilising influence, I can't help thinking that our *maiores*, our ancestors, would have spared themselves and us a lot of trouble if they'd remained within the perimeter of the Alban Hills. In that way the rest of the world could have got on with doing what it does best, *videlicet*, slitting their own throats unimpeded by the rule of law. The task of building and repairing roads, diverting rivers, constructing aqueducts, providing clean water, keeping the *plebs* entertained, maintaining law and order, settling disputes, protecting the borders, and generally ensuring that things tick over so that everyone else can relax is an interminable undertaking, and, let's face it, we get precious little thanks for it. I sometimes ask myself what it's all in aid of. Apart from the prestige of being top nation, it's a constant uphill struggle.'

And then, more obscurely: 'Aspirations…resolutions…drowned in dreams…hopeless business…unattainable laxation.'

Whereupon death clogged his eyelids, and he breathed his last.

It's an interesting fact that Caesar was the first person known to us whose body underwent an autopsy, though why the autopsy was performed is a complete mystery. It was hardly the case that the cause of death was in dispute. The autopsy was performed by his personal physician Antistius. His report read as follows:

Of the twenty-three wounds, only the second, one that was delivered to the neck, was fatal. In my professional opinion the murder was perpetrated by a bunch of rank amateurs more anxious in securing accreditation for their bloody deed than in the efficient and effective dispatch of their victim. I can't say for certain whether the victim slowly bled to death or drowned in his own blood and vomit. My main task was to sew the corpse back together. If I'd performed a more through autopsy, there would have been precious little left for burial.

The funeral procession began in the Forum outside the *regia*. The plan was to bury Caesar in his family tomb in the Campus Martius, but things got out of hand. The mourners went wild and instead set fire to his corpse in the Forum after Mark Antony had delivered his funeral oration.

Legend has it that the following note was discovered among the papers of his father-in-law Lucius Calpurnius Piso Caesoninus:

> My son-in-law at the end of his life was, as we know, a spent Colossus, whose failures equalled his successes. What once had been magnificent had become terrible, what once had been beautiful had become ugly. If anything beyond the strictly palpable constituted a part of his belief system, that something was an unshakeable belief in his own star – a star that burned alone in a pitiless firmament emptied of the gods. A supreme egotist in love with his own *dignitas*, he was prepared to die rather than deface the perfect form of his egotism.
>
> Yet though there can be no excuse for what he ultimately became, had he not been subjected to the pressures of a system that always sets out to corrupt those whom it cannot destroy, the flaws of his personality would never have grown to such malevolent proportions. The transformation of his strengths and virtues into vices and weaknesses is something for which all men of principle must share equal responsibility.
>
> One thing is certain: the world has been changed irrevocably by the man's restless and unfulfilled genius. We and our descendants are condemned in perpetuity to live out the consequences of his destructive undertakings and urges. There is not one of us who does not walk in Caesar's shade.
>
> Yet, for all his cruelty and manipulation, I would not have wished him dead. A political vacuum has been created which will attract all the most sordid elements. I very much suspect that his death will have bequeathed protracted suffering to a people who have already supped full on the horrors of civil strife. A tapestry is unravelling of which we can only take the measure of its fringe. My poor daughter, as you can imagine, is inconsolable.

Four months after Caesar's assassination, a comet appeared in the early evening sky just as spectators were pouring out of an amphitheatre where games were being held in honour of Venus Genetrix. The games had been sponsored by Caius Octavius, Caesar's grandnephew and now his heir. Traditionally the appearance of a comet was interpreted as a harbinger of some catastrophe such as famine, plague or war. Octavius, however, claimed that it indicated that the soul of Caesar had been received among the immortal gods. He attached a star to a statue of Caesar that stood in the Forum and minted coins depicting a star at Caesar's forehead.

As for what happened in the years that followed – the defeat of the assassins at the Battle of Philippi in Macedonia, the breakdown in the relationship between Mark Antony and Octavius, Octavius' naval victory over Mark Antony at the Battle of Actium off the north-west

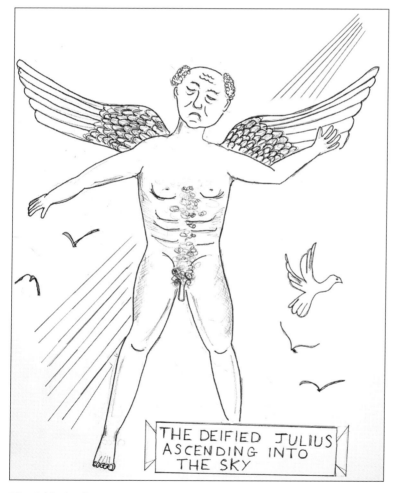

The deified Julius Caesar.

coast of Greece, and the establishment of the Principate under Augustus, by which title Octavius was known henceforth – all this is the stuff of history, rather than legend, and needs no telling here.

What is not so well known is that one of the first public acts that Augustus performed when he became *princeps* or first citizen, his technical title, was to order his priests to pronounce the building in which Caesar perished a *locus sceleratus*; that is to say, he had the room officially cursed and sealed off. Once the priests had got through with their routine, Rome's municipal workers moved in with their cement and walled the place up.

THE GREAT GOD PAN IN THE LATRINE

Pan eases himself in a Roman latrine.

That wasn't the end of the story, however. About a century later the authorities decided that the building was too prime a piece of real estate to leave permanently out of commission. They knocked down the wall that had closed it off, had the priests repeat the same ritual in reverse to uncurse it, and converted the space into a public latrine. The jovial fellowship of a house of defecation thus became a fitting coda to a life that had been subject to an unpredictable fundament.

There's one last legend I can't resist telling. In 410 CE Alaric the Visigoth was besieging Rome. When the Emperor Honorius refused to agree to his demands, Alaric sacked the eternal city. Relative to most sacks, his, however, was relatively mild. Churches were largely spared, as were their contents. Even so, Rome had not been sacked for 800 years – the last occasion was by the Gauls – and the event sent major shock waves through the empire. Honorius, too, experienced palpitations when he heard the news – but not because of the city. He thought that the messenger, who happened to be the keeper of his poultry, was referring to his pet chicken.

His pet chicken happened to be called Roma.

Honour thy gods.
Practice moderation.
Keep your enemies far from you.
Extol virtue.
Respect the dead.

Further Reading

Modern Studies

Controversy rages over the historical basis for the legends of early Rome. A. Fraschetti, *The Foundation of Rome* (Edinburgh UP, 2002), argues that Romulus was invented by the Romans to account for their imperial destiny, whereas Andrea Carandini, *Rome: Day One* (Princeton UP, 2011), claims on the basis of archaeological evidence that Rome was indeed founded by Romulus. G. Forsythe, *A Critical History of Early Rome: From Prehistory to the First Punic War* (Univ. of California Press, 2005), provides a detailed introduction to the history. R. Ross Holloway *The Archaeology of Early Rome and Latium* (Routledge, 1994), offers a critical introduction to the complex issues surrounding the regal period. Many of the legends have received detailed treatment. T.P. Wiseman, *Remus: A Roman Myth* (Cambridge UP, 1995), investigates how Romulus came to acquire a twin brother and why he was killed at the moment of Rome's foundation. His *Roman Drama and Roman History* (Univ. of Exeter Press, 1998) argues for connections between the origins of Roman historiography and dramatic performances. The legends of Romulus and of the abduction or rape of the Sabines are discussed in G. Miles, *Livy: Reconstructing Early Rome* (Cornell UP, 1997), and in E. Dench, *Romulus' Asylum: Roman Identities from the Age of Alexander to the Age of Hadrian* (Oxford UP, 2005). T. Cornell, 'Coriolanus' (pp. 73–97 in *History and Culture in Republican Rome: Studies in Honour of T.P. Wiseman*, ed. D. Braund and C. Gill (Edinburgh UP, 2003), sees the myth of Coriolanus as being exemplary of both virtues and defects in the Roman character. Jaclyn Neel, *Legendary Rivals: Collegiality and Ambition in the Tales of Early Rome* (Brill, 2015), argues that many of the elements of Rome's early legends were influenced by the social and political conditions of the late Republic, particularly the civil war period (43–30 BCE). T.P. Wiseman's *The Myth of Rome* (Univ. of Exeter

Press, 2004) offers a scholarly but highly readable refutation of the now discredited claim that the Romans lacked a mythic imagination, while also demonstrating the profound impact of Roman myth on writers, politicians, thinkers, artists, etc. Best of all by way of introduction to the whole debate about the relationship between myth and history are the first hundred and thirty pages of M. Beard, *S.P.Q.R.: A History of Ancient Rome* (W.W. Norton & Co., 2015). For the downfall of the Republic, I recommend Tom Holland's *Rubicon: The Triumph and Tragedy of the Roman Republic* (Doubleday, 2003), well-researched but intended for the general reader.

Ancient Sources in Translation

Livy, *The Early History of Rome (Books I–V)*. Translated by Aubrey de Sélincourt (Penguin Classics, 2005).

Livy, *The History of Rome (Books 1–5)*. Translated by Valerie Warrior with introduction and Notes (Hackett Publishing Company, 2006).

Livy, *The Rise of Rome: Books One to Five*. Translated by T. J. Luce (Oxford World Classics, 2009).

Plutarch, *Makers of Rome*. Translated by I. Scott-Kilvert (Penguin Classics, 1965).

Vergil, *The Aeneid*. Translated by Sarah Ruden (Yale University Press, 2008).

Vergil, *The Aeneid*. Translated by Shadi Bartsch (Profile Books, 2020).

Virgil, *The Aeneid*. Translated by Robert Fitzgerald (Vintage Classics, 1960).

Virgil, *The Aeneid*. Translated by Robert Fagles with Introduction by Bernard Knox (Penguin Classics, 2010).

Virgil, *The Aeneid*. Translated by David Ferry (The University of Chicago Press, 2017).